Married To Money

Van & Lolita Brown

ISBN: 979-8-9989579-1-8

Imprint: Independently published.

Printed in the United States of America

DEDICATION

We give gratitude and honor to our Heavenly Father.
I pray that our lives reflect the vision you have for us.

May this book inspire and lead our children to Kingdom success.
Your lives has radically enriched ours. Love you too
much Ezekiel, Zayna and Ziza.

To the multitude that will encounter this book. May God grant the knowledge, wisdom and understanding to live out these ideals.

THE INTENTION BEHIND THE COVER

Every element of the *Married to Money* cover was chosen with intention because this book itself is intentional. Nothing is accidental. Nothing is loud. Everything is aligned.

At the center stand two vessels, positioned side by side. They are different in form, yet they share the same ground, the same posture, and the same direction. This is the visual language of partnership. Marriage was never designed to be a competition of roles or a pursuit of sameness, but an agreement of purpose.

The taller vessel, finished in a soft ivory tone, represents structure, vision, and leadership. It reflects steadiness, the kind that builds, protects, and thinks forward. It speaks to responsibility and direction, to the quiet strength required to carry vision over time.

Beside it rests a rounded terracotta vessel, symbolic of nurture, flow, and stewardship. This vessel represents the ability to receive, hold, multiply, and sustain what has been entrusted. It reflects wisdom in management, discernment in timing, and the grace required to steward growth without waste.

Together, these vessels tell a truth many couples miss: alignment matters more than equality. When purpose is shared, difference becomes strength.

Beneath them lies a stone and a detail of wheat. The stone speaks to foundation, stability formed over time, wisdom earned through consistency, not impulse. The wheat represents provision, growth, and biblical abundance. It reminds us that wealth is cultivated. It grows slowly. It responds to patience, faith, and obedience. Notice that money is never displayed, because real wealth does not need to announce itself. It reveals itself through fruit.

A small brass bowl sits nearby, modest in size and intentional in presence. It represents capacity: what we choose to receive, save, give, and manage wisely. Its restraint is deliberate. True wealth always begins with discipline before expansion. Preparedness comes before abundance.

The entire scene is surrounded by a warm, soft glow, almost like a quiet halo. It represents divine alignment. Not excess. Not striving. But intentionality. It suggests that marriage and money, when handled correctly, are sacred responsibilities. Money is not worshipped here. It is stewarded.

The linen fabrics and earth-toned textures ground the image

in humility and labor. They speak to timelessness. To legacy. To the understanding that wealth is built slowly through consistent decisions, and that what lasts is rarely loud.

Even the typography reflects this posture. Calm. Centered. Spacious. It does not shout. It does not persuade. It reads like a vow, not a pitch.

Without saying a word, the cover tells the story this book exists to tell:

Wealth flows where alignment lives.

Legacy grows where stewardship is honored.

And marriage, when rooted in purpose, becomes the most powerful financial partnership there is.

CONTENTS

INTRODUCTION

How Did I Get Here?

Van Brown's Story

I woke up startled, by far one of the scariest moments of my life. I was sleeping in my car, and a stranger was trying to break in. As I sat up, shaken, I asked myself a question that would begin to reshape everything: How did I get here?

Every human being will one day have to ask themselves a set of questions in order to become the best version of themselves. And for me to fully understand why I was sleeping in a car, being jolted awake by an intruder, I had to trace it back. I had to go deep.

I grew up in a household with six siblings. My father had other children who didn't live with us. My mother worked as a caregiver, and my father drove for the local telecommunications company. He was a creature of habit, up at 7:00 AM like clockwork, gone until nightfall. My mother was much the same. They worked hard. Very hard.

We had bills, but there was never any conversation about them. I saw envelopes on the table, I saw lights on, and somehow, things got paid. But no one ever said how. No one taught us. There were no family talks about money. All I knew was that things were tight.

We wore hand-me-downs. I showed up to school with shoes and uniforms that invited jokes, not compliments. And kids in public school, especially inner-city schools, can be relentless. Lunchtime was often hit or miss. And when we had nothing, we just dealt with it. But those moments, those stingy, embarrassing, gut-hollowing moments, planted something in me. My brothers and I got tired of it. Tired of the teasing. Tired of the lack. So we started working, washing cars, selling fruit, and painting houses just to afford a piece of dignity.

I'll never forget the first time I bought my own pair of jeans, Lee Jeans. That brand was everything to me back then. I was proud. I finally felt like I belonged. And those British Knights on my feet? Man, I felt like royalty. We even started helping our sisters by buying them uniforms, shoes, the works, because they too were targets. We were trying to make up for something that wasn't our fault. But here's the real question:

How did my parents get there?

With all their hard work, how did we still come up short? The truth is, they did what they knew. And what they knew wasn't much when it came to intentional conversations around purpose, wealth, and generational legacy, so we inherited silence where we needed strategy.

Once we could earn for ourselves, the teasing stopped. But something strange happened, I began to overspend. I bought things I didn't need simply because I could. And why? Because I was still trying to silence the voices of the bullies who mocked me as a child.

But why was no one thinking beyond survival? Why weren't we taught about money, purpose, and legacy? Why wasn't there a class in school that prepared us for the real test, the test of managing the most valuable resource we'd ever have: our purpose?

Let me be clear, I'm not angry. I'm awakened. And I'm asking you now:

- Are you where your mistakes took you, or where you're purposed for?
- Are you planted in the right place?
- Are you frustrated in your job?
- Do you count down the seconds until your shift ends?
- Would you do what you're doing now if you weren't getting paid?
- Would you want your children to follow in your exact footsteps?

These are the questions that changed my life. Because one day,

I realized I never truly chose my life. I copied it. And if your foundation is built on error, every step that follows will also be misaligned. I took jobs just to stay afloat: gas stations, hotels, malls, gyms, car services. It wasn't about discovering my purpose; it was about outrunning my bills. I didn't ask myself the right questions until my late twenties. But if I had, it would have saved me years of delay.

So now, I ask you: Is there something inside of you that you're not yet aware of?

Let me tell you how delusional I was. I thought I was going to be an athlete, a superstar. I mistook passion for purpose. But now I know purpose is the thing that, when you give it to the world, it will never forget you. The greatest tragedy in life is not death. It is living without ever discovering why you were born. Every human being is a rich solution looking for a problem to solve. And once you find it, you'll write books about it. You'll start businesses. You'll create change. But many of us were raised on tile, never exposed to the soil, the sun, and the water we needed to grow. And instead of being inspired by our hardships, we settled for survival.

We never dreamed.

Some of you had the opposite problem. You had too much, too soon. No one taught you how to manage it, so you squandered it. And now, you're lost, not because of lack, but because of luxury without leadership. Whether you were raised in poverty or privilege, the question still remains: How did you get here? And now, more importantly: Where are you going?

This isn't a blame game. This is an invitation. An invitation to ask yourself the hard questions. To stop playing it safe. To reject the limitations of the past and embrace the greatness that's been buried inside of you. Because when you stop chasing money and start pursuing purpose, money becomes a byproduct, not the pursuit. So I ask you, again:

1. How did you get here?
2. Are you playing it safe?
3. Who taught you about money and purpose?
4. Would you choose the life you're living if no one else had chosen it for you?

This is your wake-up call.

This is the beginning of your return.

This is the moment you stop existing… and start living.

Lolita Brown's Story

As far back as I can remember, my mother would often tell the story of when I was just a baby or small child. She would take me to stores and various outings, and strangers, completely unprovoked, would stop her and say, "That's a million-dollar baby. She's just so beautiful." Unbeknownst to my mother or me at the time, they were prophetically speaking into my destiny, declaring what God had already ordained for my life.

I'm the youngest of ten children. My mother, recognizing something unique in me, did her best to shelter and guide me. She placed me in private and Catholic schools, striving to provide me with the best education possible. No matter what sacrifices she had to make personally, she made sure I never went without. She gave me the best of everything, even when it cost her deeply.

Naturally, I found my way into the real estate industry at a young age. I began as an escrow officer, eventually became a loan processor, and later managed an entire escrow department. That season of my life was my first encounter with true success and real income. Between my earnings and an inheritance I received, I began to live freely, perhaps too freely. I had a place in Palos Verdes simply because I wanted to wake up to the sight of dolphins in the ocean. I had another place in Downtown LA near a warehouse I managed. I traveled, shopped, and lived extravagantly, all without understanding the value of money. All I knew was that it came to me easily and frequently.

Then came 2007. The market crash shook me to my core. It was devastating, but in hindsight, it was also the beginning of my purpose. That breaking point became the birthplace of my calling. Had I known then what I know now, I would have embraced that season rather than feared it. Even meeting my husband is tied to that journey. We crossed paths while I was walking in my purpose.

At one point, I went from managing multiple properties to moving back in with my mother, sleeping in the same room I had during high school. I had to restructure my finances and focus on simply paying bills. That's when one of my dearest friends called me and said, "I want to talk to you about a business opportunity in the financial industry." My first thought was, "I don't need to know anything about money. I don't have any!" But she said something that stayed with me forever: "You don't plan to stay there, do you?" I said no. And she replied, "Then don't plan for where you are. Plan for where you want to be."

That one statement was the spark I needed. I got off the couch, drove hours to a presentation, and sat in a room learning about money management, investing, and building a business. Initially, I had no intention of working in finance. I just wanted to learn how to manage my own money better. After having made so much and having nothing to show for it, I realized I needed to become a good steward. I wanted to break generational cycles and build something lasting for those connected to me.

As I immersed myself in the firm, something shifted. I developed a genuine passion for helping others transform their financial lives. Watching people go from having no savings and no plan to building wealth, eliminating debt, buying homes, and preparing for retirement ignited something in me. Helping others develop a wealthy mindset became my mission.

Eighteen years later, I'm still in this field. That one decision opened the door to my business, Manage My Wealth, and led to building a ministry and legacy alongside my husband. I met him at that very financial firm. He walked in looking for guidance on his portfolio and walked out with me. Together, we now serve couples, families, and individuals at every stage, from those just beginning their journey to those who are already established and ready to grow together.

If you're stuck in a cycle of earning, spending, and starting over, or if you're ready to multiply what you already have, this book is for you.

Whether you're managing money with your spouse, your children, or your community, I pray this book pulls out the seed of purpose that's already inside of you. The harvest is waiting.

My beginning was a mix of blessings and blind spots. Success came quickly, but so did loss. Poor stewardship, lack of knowledge, and inexperience cost me dearly. But I believe that God never wastes a moment. Every detour became divine direction. And now, with wisdom, strategy, and grace, I am honored to teach others not just how to manage their wealth, but how to multiply it and leave it as a legacy.

CHAPTER ONE

THE SPIRITUAL BLUEPRINT FOR A PURPOSEFUL LIFE

Lolita Brown

There is a peace that settles deep in your soul when you truly understand this: Nothing belongs to you. Everything belongs to God. Your house, your car, your children, your business, your marriage, even the breath in your lungs, has been entrusted to you by a loving Father. You are not the owner. You are the steward. Once this revelation takes root, it releases you from the weight of ownership and the pressure of trying to control outcomes that were never meant to be in your hands to begin with.

This is the foundation Van and I built our marriage upon. Very early in our journey together, we came into agreement that we were not just husband and wife, but heirs to a rightful throne. As children of God, everything in our possession is on loan from our Heavenly Father. Our role is to manage it well.

This spiritual foundation shaped how we viewed our finances. Money wasn't something to chase or hoard. It was a tool, given by God, to fulfill the assignment He placed on our lives.

From Ownership to Stewardship

When you shift from an ownership mentality to a stewardship mindset, everything changes. Ownership says, "This is mine. I have to make it work. I have to provide." Stewardship says, "God, You've placed this in my hands. Show me how to manage it for Your glory." With that mindset, the pressure to perform, strive, and provide lifts. Instead, you become a co-laborer with God, partnering with Him to steward His resources well.

For Van and I, this looked very practical. We sat down and created strategies together. We asked God for wisdom on how to manage what He had given us. We didn't start with the bank account. We started with our hearts. Our conversations were rooted in prayer, asking, "*Lord, how would You have us handle what belongs to You*?"

The Spiritual Skill Set of a Good Manager

Being a good steward doesn't happen by accident. It requires intentionality. There are spiritual and practical skills you must cultivate:

Discipline: Staying consistent even when it's inconvenient.

Strategy: Having a clear plan for the resources entrusted to you.

Foresight & Insight: Seeing beyond the moment, preparing for what's ahead.

Care & Responsibility: Honoring what's been placed in your hands.

We understood that without discipline and divine strategy, we would mismanage what God had entrusted to us. And mismanagement always leads to loss. Every time we slipped into the mindset of "this is ours," we found ourselves stressed, overwhelmed, and losing ground, whether in relationships, investments, or business opportunities. When we took ownership instead of stewardship, we carried burdens we were never designed to bear. But when we returned to our foundation, that it all belongs to God, we found peace, clarity, and favor.

Learning to Let Go

One of the hardest lessons for me personally was learning to let go.

Letting go of relationships.

Letting go of failed investments.

Letting go of my own expectations.

God had to remind me: *"Lolita, if I gave it, I can take it. Trust Me in the taking, just as you trust Me in the giving."*

Releasing control allowed me to grow in faith and develop a deeper trust in God's provision. Every closed door became an opportunity to realign with His plan.

Building with God's Blueprint

Our shared spiritual foundation also gave us prophetic clarity. We didn't make major decisions without seeking God's direction. When we were buying our first home, we didn't know where to begin. So we sat, prayed, and meditated. I remember specifically asking God to show us the house, even down to the address. I wanted it to reflect something meaningful, like a number from our wedding day. Sure enough, when we found our home, those numbers were in the address. That was God's signature. These moments became milestones of our faith, affirming that as long as we stayed connected to Him, we would always be provided for.

The Financial Scriptures That Anchored Us

To keep our hearts and minds aligned, we surrounded ourselves with the Word. We chose five scriptures that spoke to stewardship, financial growth, and work ethic. We posted them around the house, on mirrors, in the kitchen, and down the hallway. Every time we passed them, we recited them out loud. This constant reminder wasn't about superstition. It was about alignment. It kept our focus on God as our Source, not the world.

Your Wealth Is Already Assigned

Here's a truth that will set you free: God has already ordained the resources you need to fulfill your assignment. He knew the purpose He placed on your life before you were formed. He knows the exact amount of wealth, influence, and resources required to accomplish it. You don't have to strive for it. You have to manage what's been given and align with His timing.

When we chase money for money's sake, we get out of alignment. But when we focus on fulfilling God's purpose, provision follows. The money is already assigned to your name. The question is not, "Will I get it?" but, "Am I ready to manage it well?" The more you develop as a good steward, the faster God can release what's already yours.

Walking It Out in Peace

It's not about competition. It's about ***manifestation****.*

Every idea, every dream you believe you came up with was planted by God. Your job is to cultivate it, manage it, and trust Him for the increase. When you understand that, the stress of finances lifts, and you can walk in peace knowing you are in divine partnership with the One who owns it all. When we stay rooted in this shared spiritual foundation, we find joy in the journey, whether we're building a business, raising a family, or navigating financial decisions.

Van and I are anchored in this truth: "*We are stewards, not owners. And our Father is faithful to supply.*"

Van Brown

If two people are going to build a life together, whether it's a marriage, a business, or a legacy, it only makes sense that they start with the same foundation. Without it, they are bound to face unnecessary turbulence. Two individuals with opposing worldviews will always interpret life's challenges differently. This misalignment guarantees constant friction, different outcomes, and ultimately, division.

Take a look at our society today. Look at the polarization in our nation. In recent elections, families have been torn apart over political views. Social media is flooded with stories of siblings, parents, and lifelong friends cutting ties simply because they voted differently. Why? Because their foundational beliefs about life, leadership, and morality are not aligned. If political ideologies can divide families so easily, imagine what happens when two people in a marriage, who are supposed to be one, have opposing spiritual foundations. The impact is far greater.

Your spiritual life is your compass. It determines how you receive information, how you process adversity, and how you make decisions. If one person is rooted in the world's systems, believing life "just happens," while the other is anchored in the truth that God created them for a divine purpose, they will never navigate life the same way. The storms of life will come. One will crumble, while the other will stand firm.

You see, if you believe your life belongs to you, you'll approach every situation through a lens of self-preservation and self-glory. But if you know you are merely a steward of what God has entrusted to you, your time, your gifts, and your resources, then your decisions will reflect that higher calling.

Everything You Love Has a Creator

Pause and consider this: Every valuable thing you own, your car, your phone, your home, was created by someone. And when it breaks, you don't expect it to fix itself. You return to the manufacturer. You consult the manual. You seek the source. If your iPhone glitches, it cannot repair itself. You call Apple. If your car breaks down, you call the mechanic, not the car. So why is it so hard for people to believe that human beings have a Creator? And if we do, wouldn't it make sense to consult Him for guidance on how to navigate life, marriage, and yes, even money?

God will never force you to follow Him. He won't save you from your choices. If pride, narcissism, or worldly philosophies are your companions, He will allow you to walk with them. But if you truly recognize Him as your Creator, you'll understand the necessity of being equally yoked with a partner who honors that same truth.

Words Can Be Misleading, Look for Evidence

It's easy for someone to say, "I'm a Christian." But in the courtroom of life, statements are not enough. The world, like a good judge, demands evidence. Don't just ask a potential spouse or business partner what they believe. Look for proof. What has their obedience to God produced? When was the last time they heard God, acted on His instruction, and bore fruit from it? Saying you're a believer but living without evidence is like owning a toolbox and not knowing how to use a single tool inside. Useless. A wrench, a screwdriver, and a drill only become valuable when used with understanding and purpose.

The Danger of Convenience Connections

Many relationships today are built on convenience, not calling. People are drawn to silhouettes, charm, and status, but neglect to ask the most critical question: Does this person's spiritual foundation align with where God is taking me? Not every beautiful woman is meant to walk with you. Not every successful man is equipped to build with you. Compatibility in the natural means little if there is no compatibility in the spirit.

Remember: *foundation is everything.*

Prayer: The Connection to Source

Let's shift to an even deeper revelation. Prayer is not a religious obligation. It's a lifeline. Think of it as your software update. Tech companies continually send updates to keep your devices running smoothly, not because they love you, but because they value their name. God does the same. He downloads wisdom, correction, and new strategies through prayer, not because He needs to, but because His name is on you. You are His creation. Staying connected to Him ensures you function at your highest capacity.

Yet many of us only pray when crisis hits. We've reduced God to a wealthy uncle we call on when in need. But relationships don't thrive on emergency contact. They thrive on consistency. The more you stay in communion with God, the better you navigate life. Challenges won't disappear, but your response to them will be different. Your response will be rooted in peace and guided by His voice.

Marrying Money, But with Purpose

Now, let's bring this into the context of finances. Money itself isn't evil. It's a tool. But how you approach it reveals your foundation. A couple who sees money through the lens of stewardship, understanding it all belongs to God, will handle wealth with wisdom. They won't be tossed by greed, pride, or fear. On the other hand, if one person views money as power and the other as a tool for purpose, you're going to have constant conflict. It's not a money problem. It's a foundation problem. The same applies to business, investments, and even raising children. If your values are not aligned, every decision becomes a battleground.

Every idea, every product, every system started in the mind of a creator. You are no different. You were created with intention. And staying connected to your Creator is what unlocks your full potential. So before you merge your life, your name, and your finances with another person, make sure your foundations are aligned, not by words, but by evidence. Because when life gets hard, and it will, you'll need someone who knows how to stand firm, not someone who gets swept away by the winds of culture. Foundation isn't optional. It's everything.

Reflection Questions:

1. Does my current relationship, or potential relationship, reflect evidence of a shared spiritual foundation, or is it built on convenience and emotion?

____

____

____

____

2. In what ways have I personally sought God's guidance for my financial decisions?

____

____

____

____

3. Do I treat prayer as a lifeline to stay connected with my Creator, or as a last resort in times of trouble?

____

____

____

____

4. Am I aligned with someone whose spiritual compass will help us navigate life's storms with clarity and unity?

____

____

____

____

Chapter Two

UNITING IN PURPOSE AND FINDING YOUR JOINT MISSION

Lolita Brown

Marriage is more than love. It is more than passion. It is more than two people deciding to share a home, a last name, and a bed. Marriage, at least the kind that thrives, is a partnership with a purpose.

When a husband and wife come together with a shared vision, they create a force that is not easily broken. That vision becomes the compass, the anchor, and the fuel. And when that vision is rooted in God's purpose, it draws wealth, not just for the sake of money itself, but for mission. Wealth without mission is wasted potential, but wealth with mission is unstoppable.

When my husband and I first met, we didn't know the full scope of what God was orchestrating between us. But as we grew closer, we began to discover shared threads. We both dreamed of starting an international nonprofit. We both had a deep desire to help couples navigate marital challenges. We both wanted to see people free from financial bondage and lifted out of poverty. Those weren't just nice ideas; they were God-planted seeds. When we married, God made it clear: this was not just about the two of us. He had joined us for an assignment. And once we recognized that, things began to align.

The day we secured our 501(c)(3) status, it was a spiritual turning point. We weren't just two individuals chasing separate goals anymore; we were two people committed to one vision. That vision gave us the ambition to stay disciplined, the focus to keep moving forward, and the determination to build something that would outlive us. You see, when you unite in marriage with a clear mission, you give wealth a purpose in your life. God doesn't send you here empty-handed. He plants your purpose within you before you take your first breath. And along with that purpose comes every resource you'll need to fulfill it.

Here's the truth: there is already a portion of wealth assigned to your life. It's not random, and it's not equal for everyone. It's directly tied to your purpose. When you start identifying that purpose, even if all you have is a glimpse, you begin unlocking what I call your "heavenly bank account." Suddenly, you're not just working for money; money is working for your mission. Once my husband and I understood that, our entire approach to money shifted. We stopped treating it like something to chase and started treating it like something to direct.

We created a plan: short-term savings, mid-term savings, long-term savings, and a dedicated sowing account for giving.

These weren't just financial buckets; they were vehicles for our mission. Because here's the thing about money: it's currency. It flows. It moves constantly, 24/7. The question is: do you have the systems, skills, and purpose to attract it and direct it when it comes?

The world's financial systems, including banking, investments, and real estate, were never flawed in their design. The problem is that corruption crept in through people. But if we, as couples, can return to God's original intent for these systems and apply them to our family's financial strategy, we can build generational wealth and steward it well. Unfortunately, I see many couples operating with divided visions, separate goals, separate finances, and separate missions. A divided house cannot stand, and a divided marriage cannot maximize its wealth potential. When you move as one, you position yourself for the blessing. When you're united, God can pour into your household without blockage.

It's not about whose paycheck is bigger or who handles which bills. It's about acknowledging that everything is stewarded by the two of you and ultimately belongs to God. The question becomes: How will we manage this together? How will we steward the house, the children, the car, the investments, and the opportunities He's entrusted to us?

My husband and I have a personal rule: we never see ourselves as owners of what God has given us, only managers. Our goal is always to take what He's entrusted to us, grow it, and return it to Him better than it came. That mindset changes everything. Unity doesn't happen by accident. It's built through intentional conversations. One talk about vision at the beginning of your marriage isn't enough. You need regular check-ins. Circumstances shift. Economies change. Opportunities evolve. You have to be willing to pivot together without losing sight of the bigger mission.

And here's a principle I've learned from the wealthiest people I've ever worked with: they are quick to make a decision and slow to change it. They understand that opportunities often require swift discernment, but they also understand the danger of abandoning course too quickly when emotions get involved. Couples, adopt that discipline. Decide together. Commit together. And when challenges come, and they will, face them as a team, not as opponents.

It's not "you versus me."

It's "us versus the problem."

And when you have that mindset, when you truly operate as one, your vision will not just build wealth. It will build legacy.

Van Brown

If we want to be successful in life and in marriage, we must first agree on something fundamental: God did not design marriage simply for companionship, romance, or personal fulfillment, although these are beautiful fruits of it. He designed marriage as a joint mandate. It is His way of uniting two distinct individuals into one mission so that His purpose on the earth can be accomplished through their unity.

This means that while you are complete in yourself and capable of living independently, marriage, when ordained by God, has an assignment attached to it. And if that is true, then it is no surprise why the enemy works so tirelessly to dismantle and distract couples. He is not simply after your happiness; he is after your collaboration. He knows that if he can derail the joint task, he can weaken the very structure that holds communities, nations, and ultimately the world together.

The breakdown of marriage is not just a domestic issue. It is a societal one. Think about it. If we want a healthy world, we need healthy continents. For healthy continents, we need healthy nations. For healthy nations, we need healthy states. For healthy states, we need healthy cities. For healthy cities, we need healthy neighborhoods. And at the root of healthy neighborhoods are healthy marriages.

When you picture the most beautiful, peaceful neighborhood you'd love to live in, chances are it's a place where families are intact, neighbors are kind, and there's a sense of safety and order. That is not by accident. It is the ripple effect of unity at the most intimate level: the home. Everything about God's design speaks order, structure, and unity. But the world has sold us a different vision, one that celebrates self over covenant.

Social media thrives on the selfie. The culture encourages us to "speak our truth" and "say what you feel," which is fine if you intend to live entirely for yourself. But in a joint mandate like marriage, unity depends on being equally yoked. Success in marriage is not built on feelings alone. It is built on vision, discipline, and agreement.

When God said, "For this reason a man shall leave his father and mother and be joined to his wife" (Genesis 2:24), He was not simply making a poetic statement about romance. He was making a declaration about priority. In marriage, your spouse becomes the most important person in your life. It's not your parents, not your in-laws, not your friends, and not your past.

And have you ever wondered why the Bible specifies the man leaving, but does not say the same about the woman? The answer lies in understanding the nature of fatherhood. The word "father" means source, sustainer, provider. In the traditional wedding, when a father walks his daughter down the aisle, he is symbolically saying: I have sourced you, sustained you, and provided for you. Now I transfer that responsibility to your husband. It is a handover of stewardship, not a loss of identity.

When we understand roles, unity becomes natural. The wife is called a helper in Scripture, not in a lesser sense, but as one who brings strength to fulfill the mission. And while each of us will always have personal callings from God, the marriage mandate exists because there is something God wants done that can only be accomplished together.

If your spouse is the most important person in your life, then that priority must be guarded. No one should have the freedom to speak against them in your presence, whether in jest or criticism. If you have to choose a side, you stand with your spouse, not out of blind loyalty, but because God Himself joined you together for His purpose. Here's the beauty: when you both know the vision and mandate God has given you, it naturally shapes your words, your tone, your conflict resolution, and the way you cover each other in weakness. Purpose disciplines behavior.

Consider the athlete who, from childhood, is told they are destined for the Olympics. Because they see their future so clearly, they say no to drugs, destructive habits, and distractions, not because they are rules to follow, but because those things have no place in their destiny. Joseph was the same way. When Potiphar's wife tempted him, he refused, not just because it was wrong, but because it had nothing to do with where God was taking him. And when God elevated him, he didn't waste time getting revenge. He was too busy fulfilling his assignment. Too often in marriage, we let offense and ego derail the mandate. We use our successes to prove a point to our past instead of using them to glorify God. That is a sign our motivation was never love or purpose, but vengeance.

In a true marriage mandate, you guard your words, not because you walk on eggshells, but because you are stewarding God's work. You communicate, resolve conflict, and refuse to go silent when things get hard. You stay present because you understand the weight of what God has entrusted to you.

But here is the truth: You cannot bring unity to your marriage if you are not unified within yourself. Your private life determines how you show up in crisis. You need a personal relationship with God that is independent of your spouse. Time in prayer, fasting, and meditation where you hear from Him directly. Corporate prayer is powerful, but God also wants you alone.

Think of it like a phone or laptop. No matter how advanced the device, it's useless without being plugged into power. God is your source. Every time you plug in through prayer and intimacy with Him, you gain strength, clarity, and capacity to love your spouse well.

When both husband and wife cultivate that private devotion, the marriage becomes unstoppable. Unity deepens. Tenderness increases. God's projects on the earth get accomplished. So here is my encouragement: Make space for God in your private life. Fast once a week on your own. Spend 30 minutes a day in personal prayer. Take moments throughout the day to meditate on His Word. Encourage your spouse to do the same. And watch how your personal connection to God becomes the foundation for your unity together.

Because when God joins two people, He is not just creating a home; He is commissioning a mission. And the success of that mission will always begin in the secret place.

Chapter Three

FAITH & FINANCES: TRUSTING GOD WITH YOUR MONEY

Lolita Brown

Money is one of the greatest tests in marriage. It is not just about paying bills, buying homes, or planning for the future, it is about trust. Trust in God, trust in your spouse, and trust in the principles that govern kingdom wealth. For me, understanding these principles did not come overnight. I had always been a giver. From a young age, I gave to family, friends, and anyone who had a need. But giving out of kindness is not the same thing as sowing in the Spirit. For years, I lacked the revelation of what tithing and sowing really meant.

My First Lesson in Tithing

When I first started dating my husband, I had just received a large sum of money. Naturally, I wanted to give, but the amount I gave was far less than a tithe. My husband gently pulled me aside. He wasn't harsh, he wasn't condemning, he simply began to teach me.

He explained that a tithe is not a random gift; it is a divine principle. The word "tithe" means tenth. It is the first ten percent of all our increase, returned back to God. Malachi 3:10 says, "Bring the whole tithe into the storehouse, that there may be food in my house. Test me in this," says the LORD Almighty, "and see if I will not throw open the floodgates of heaven and pour out so much blessing that there will not be room enough to store it."

He helped me see that when we tithe, we are not paying God a bill, we are acknowledging Him as our Source. It is an act of covenant. Tithing places God first in our finances and opens the door for His protection and blessing. That conversation marked me. It was the first time I truly saw money as spiritual. It wasn't just about generosity, it was about obedience. It was about trusting God with what was already His.

Tithes, Offerings & Sowing

As we grew together, I began to understand the difference between tithing, offering, and sowing.

Tithe – The first 10% of your income, holy and set apart unto God. It is not optional. It belongs to Him.

Offering – Anything given beyond the tithe, often to bless a ministry, church, or mission. Offerings flow from gratitude and love.

Sowing – A Spirit-led act of planting seed into specific ground, often tied to prophetic instruction or faith for a future harvest.

Sowing is not casual giving, it is targeted, faith-driven giving.

Creating a Lifestyle of Sowing

As a couple, one of the practical things my husband and I decided to do was establish a sowing account. Scripture tells us, "God gives seed to the sower" (2 Corinthians 9:10). We wanted to be intentional about always having seed available when the Holy Spirit prompted us to give.

Too often, people misunderstand this principle. I have watched some give recklessly, even using rent money as a "seed," and then struggle when their bills come due. But biblical sowing is not reckless, it is responsible, Spirit-led stewardship. God never asks us to abandon wisdom. He sees us in our fullness, our responsibilities, our needs, and our future, and He honors good stewardship.

By setting up a separate account for sowing, we created space for God to move without creating unnecessary financial strain. Now, when an opportunity arises, we don't give in fear or confusion. We go to that account, pray together, and ask, "Lord, what portion of this seed do You want us to release?"

Spirit-Led Giving

Sometimes the Lord will prompt us to give a portion. Other times, He may ask us to release the entire account. I remember only once in our marriage when the Lord clearly told us to sow everything we had set aside. Most of the time, He directs us to give in measure because He knows what we need to take care of and what we can release by faith.

The key is to let the Holy Spirit lead. Whether it's $500 or $500,000, sowing is about obedience, not the size of the amount. When we follow His leading, the harvest always comes, sometimes in unexpected ways, sometimes in supernatural timing.

The Blessing of Designation

This principle of designated sowing has blessed us tremendously. We have been on both sides, givers and receivers, and each time, God has proven Himself faithful. Having a sowing account removes pressure, brings clarity, and builds discipline. When you designate a portion of your income to sowing, monthly, quarterly, or yearly, you are saying to God, "I am not just a consumer. I am a sower." And God honors that.

Unity & Accountability in Marriage

Another blessing of this practice is accountability. Financial unity is critical in marriage. One spouse should not be giving behind the other's back or making rash financial decisions. By having a sowing account, both partners are included in the process. You can look at what has been set aside, pray together, and decide together.

This agreement matters. Jesus said, "If two of you agree on earth concerning anything they ask, it will be done for them by My Father in heaven" (Matthew 18:19). Agreement in giving multiplies the blessing.

Action Step for Couples

Here is my challenge to you:

1. Set up a sowing account. Decide on a consistent portion of your income to deposit into it.
2. Pray together before sowing. Invite the Holy Spirit into the decision-making process.
3. Release in faith. Don't give in fear or pressure. Give in obedience, with expectation.

As you do this, you'll find that your faith will grow, your financial unity will strengthen, and your testimony of provision will multiply. Trusting God with your money is not about emptying your pockets, it's about opening your hands. And when you open your hands, you make room for Him to fill them again and again.

Faith and finances go hand in hand. When you live by God's principles, tithing, offering, and sowing, you are not just managing money, you are building a marriage that trusts God fully, walks in unity, and leaves a legacy of faith.

Van Brown

Every meaningful conversation begins with clarity. Before two people can walk together, they must agree on what the words they speak truly mean. In marriage, this principle is non-negotiable.

"Can two walk together, except they be agreed?" (Amos 3:3). If a husband and wife are journeying toward one vision, then their understanding of the words shaping that vision must be the same. Otherwise, they may share a car but travel with different maps and find themselves lost along the way.

So let us begin with a simple yet profound question: *What is faith?*

Defining Faith

The dictionary defines faith as complete trust or confidence in someone or something. Useful, yes, but insufficient. Because trust can waver, and confidence can be shaken. Faith is something deeper, something language struggles to contain. The writer of Hebrews gives us the clearest definition: "*Now faith is the substance of things hoped for, the evidence of things not seen*" (Hebrews 11:1).

Faith is not mere belief. Belief admits the possibility of doubt. Faith is not simply trust. Trust, at times, can falter. Faith is more solid, more enduring. Faith is an unwavering knowing. It is the steady assurance that your life is already cradled in the hands of the Master, perfectly orchestrated for your good (Romans 8:28). It is the settled confidence that no matter how contrary circumstances appear, God's plan is intact and unfolding.

Consider the evidence of life: unpaid bills, the loss of a job, arguments that rattle the peace of a home, delays that frustrate expectations. Faith does not deny these realities, it transcends them. It says, "Yes, these things are present, but they do not have the final word. My Father has already written the end from the beginning."

This is why Scripture speaks of joy in trial: "*Count it all joy, my brothers and sisters, when you fall into various trials, knowing that the testing of your faith produces patience*" (James 1:2–3). Joy is born of faith. It is the knowing that what appears to hinder may, in fact, be positioning you. Every great man and woman of God was refined not in ease, but in crisis. Joseph's prison became his pathway to the palace (Genesis 41:14). Daniel's den became the stage for divine deliverance (Daniel 6:22). The Hebrew boys found freedom not outside the furnace, but within it (Daniel 3:25).

Faith transforms crisis into catalyst. It anchors the soul when storms rage (Hebrews 6:19). It sustains the mind when reason falters. It whispers, "Even if my God does not deliver me in this moment, He remains God, and I will not bow" (Daniel 3:18).

That is faith: the unwavering knowing that every circumstance is ultimately working for your good because it rests in the hands of a sovereign Father.

Defining Finance

Now let us turn to the other half of this conversation: finance. Webster defines finance as the management of large sums of money, particularly by governments or corporations. Accurate, perhaps, but incomplete. It captures the mechanics but misses the meaning. From a kingdom perspective, finance is not merely transactional, it is transformational. Money is not just currency; it is a gift entrusted by God. "*The earth is the Lord's, and the fullness thereof*" (Psalm 24:1). Every resource is His before it is ever ours.

Finances are the means by which God accomplishes His purposes on the earth. He cares for widows, feeds the hungry, establishes ministries, builds schools, and extends His kingdom through the resources He places in the hands of His children (James 1:27; Isaiah 58:10). What the world views as casual exchange, heaven regards as sacred stewardship.

This is why Scripture ties money to the heart: "For where your treasure is, there will your heart be also" (Matthew 6:21). If you treat finances as ordinary, you risk becoming careless. But if you treat them as assignment, you unlock the flow of abundance. Currency must flow like a river, not a reservoir. It was never meant to be hoarded, but released. And here is the key: money multiplies only in the soil God chooses. "*He gives seed to the sower and bread for food and will also increase your store of seed and enlarge the harvest of your righteousness*" (2 Corinthians 9:10).

Giving out of guilt or pressure produces little fruit. But sowing in obedience creates exponential increase. When you lend to God by giving where He directs, He obligates Himself to repay (Proverbs 19:17).

This is why tithing is so profound. "*Bring the whole tithe into the storehouse... and test Me in this,*" says the Lord Almighty, "*and see if I will not throw open the floodgates of heaven and pour out so much blessing that there will not be room enough to store it*" (Malachi 3:10).

Tithing is not about loss; it is about alignment. And it extends beyond money. A tithe of your time, for instance, is about 2 hours and 40 minutes each day. Imagine devoting that to God in prayer, study, or service. Wealth begins in the mind and spirit before it ever manifests in your hand.

The Posture of Stewardship

The deepest wisdom concerning money is found in posture. Do you see what you have as yours or as God's? Dr. Myles Munroe once told a story of a pastor whose home was burglarized. When Dr. Munroe heard the news, he said, "Thank God it was not your valuables." To most, that sounds strange. But here is the wisdom: If you believe possessions belong to you, then the burden of replacing them is yours. But if you acknowledge that they belong to God, then their restoration rests with Him.

This is what Jesus meant when He said, "Whoever can be trusted with very little can also be trusted with much… if you have not been trustworthy with worldly wealth, who will trust you with true riches?" (Luke 16:10–11). When you live as though nothing belongs to you, you are free to give, and God is free to entrust you with more.

Faith and Finances in Marriage

Now, let us bring this wisdom into the heart of marriage. One of the most destructive patterns I've observed in couples is financial secrecy: hidden accounts, concealed spending, quiet deceptions about money. These practices corrode trust, and trust is the true currency of marriage. "*Two are better than one, because they have a good return for their labor*" (Ecclesiastes 4:9). But how can two labor together if one hand is hidden from the other?

When you stood before God and vowed to be one, you made more than a promise to each other, you made a covenant with Him. That covenant cannot thrive on secrecy. Integrity must govern your financial life. If there is a purchase to be made, discuss it. If there is a desire in your heart, bring it into the light. Hiding invites suspicion, and suspicion breeds division.

Instead, make finances a place of unity. Pray together over your resources. Seek God's will together for direction. Decide together where to sow, where to save, and where to release. "*Again I say to you, that if two of you agree on earth concerning anything they ask, it will be done for them by* my *Father in* Heaven" (Matthew 18:19). When unity governs your finances, peace will govern your home.

A Higher Perspective

Faith is the unwavering knowing that God holds your life. Finances are the entrusted gift He places in your hand to fulfill His purposes. In marriage, these two must intertwine. When husband and wife stand in agreement on faith and finances, they unlock a flow that no crisis can dam. Their resources become more than numbers; they become testimonies. Every tithe, every offering, every intentional act of giving becomes a love letter to the world, signed by the Father's hand through their obedience.

So let your marriage be marked by this: an unshakable faith in God and a faithful stewardship of His resources. For when faith and finances walk hand in hand, you will find not only provision, but purpose, and not only abundance, but legacy.

CHAPTER FOUR

THE POWER OF UNITY IN MARRIAGE AND MONEY

"Can two walk together, except they be agreed?"(Amos 3:3)

Van Brown

There is a kind of power that appears in the earth when a husband and wife decide to move as one. It is not loud. It is not dramatic. It is steady. It is consistent. It is deeply spiritual. When a man and a woman come into true unity, spiritual unity, financial unity, emotional unity, heaven takes them seriously. Hell fears them. Generations after them benefit from them. And if we are going to talk honestly about money, legacy, and building anything that lasts, we must begin with this: unity is not optional in marriage. Unity is the engine.

Before we can talk about money, we must talk about marriage itself. Most couples are fighting about money, but money is only exposing something deeper. Many households are in conflict about how it is spent, who controls it, who "deserves" more of it, or who is "wasting" it. But in truth, couples are not actually arguing about dollars. They are arguing about definition. They are fighting because they never agreed on what marriage is in the first place. You cannot move in oneness if you do not first agree on what the two of you have become.

The world says marriage is a legally recognized union between two people in a personal relationship. According to that version, marriage is a contract: sign here, witnesses present, both parties willingly enter, and the state acknowledges you. There is nothing in that definition about purpose, assignment, destiny, heaven, or why God would join two lives and call them one.

But in the Kingdom of God, marriage is not defined by paperwork. It is not merely a social agreement. It is not built on, "I like you, you like me, let's try to do life together." In the Kingdom, marriage is a covenantal assignment. It is a divine partnership in which two people are joined by God for the purpose of fulfilling His will on the earth. In other words, God did not create marriage to make us feel less lonely. He created marriage to make us more effective.

Look at how God established the first marriage. Before Eve was ever brought to Adam, God dealt with Adam directly. God formed Adam from the dust of the ground, yes, but Adam himself did not come from dust. His body did. His essence came from God. Scripture records God saying, "Let us make man in our image, after our likeness," and then, "let them have dominion." God spoke to Himself. He did not pull Adam out of the sea the way He did fish. He did not pull Adam out of the dirt the way He did trees. He spoke from Himself and produced a being that carried Himself. Adam's spirit came from God's Spirit.

That alone matters for marriage. You cannot build as one if you do not first know who you are individually. Identity is the first pillar of unity. Before Adam ever had a wife, he had identity. He knew who he came from. He knew whose likeness he carried. That is why identity must come before intimacy. If a man does not know who he is, he will ask his wife to define him. If a woman does not know who she is, she will lean on her husband to validate her. That is too heavy a burden for either spouse to carry. You are not supposed to complete me. You are supposed to complement what God has already established in me.

After identity, God gave Adam presence. The Bible says God placed Adam in the Garden of Eden. Eden was not only a physical place; it was an atmosphere. The word carries the meaning of delight, open door, and place of access. Eden was a realm where heaven and earth were in open conversation. Adam did not have to pray for the presence of God because he lived in the presence of God. Before God gave Adam partnership, He established him in presence.

Then God gave Adam an assignment. "Work it and keep it," He told him. Cultivate it. Develop it. Protect it. Multiply what I have placed in your hands. Work, in the Kingdom, does not mean toil. Work means becoming what God placed inside you. When God told Adam to work, He was not telling him, "Clock in and get a check." He was telling him, "Become the expression of what

I put in you." True work is the revealing of your God-given nature, not the renting out of your energy.

This is why a man who has not yet discovered his assignment is not yet prepared for marriage. Because without assignment, he cannot cover. Without assignment, he cannot direct. Without assignment, he cannot answer, "Where are we going?"

After identity, presence, assignment, and responsibility, God gave Adam instruction. "You may eat from all these trees, but not this one." This is order, boundaries, and consecration. You cannot lead without boundaries. You cannot protect what you refuse to restrain. What you refuse to restrain, you cannot truly protect. It is only then that God says, "It is not good for man to be alone."

We must be honest here: God did not say, "It is not good for man to be alone" as a general statement about all mankind. He was not saying, "Every man needs a wife immediately." He said, "It is not good for this man," this man who is walking in identity, functioning in My likeness, standing in My presence, fulfilling My assignment, demonstrating responsibility, and obeying instruction, to be alone. In other words, this kind of man is ready for partnership.

Marriage was never meant to rescue you from loneliness. Marriage was meant to multiply what God had already started in you.

This is why I say, gently but directly, to my brothers and to my sisters: Know who you are before you offer yourself to someone else. If you don't know who you are, the person you marry will name you. And if they are broken, they will name you from a broken place. If they are insecure, they will name you from insecurity. If they are controlling, they will name you in a way that keeps you beneath them. But when both of you come into marriage already rooted in God, already submitted to His voice, and already committed to His assignment, now you are not marrying to fill a void. You are marrying to fulfill a mandate. That is why spiritual unity is not romance. It is strategy.

When God formed Eve, Scripture says He brought her to Adam. Pay attention. God did not force her on him. God presented her, and Adam recognized her. Adam said, "This is bone of my bone and flesh of my flesh." Adam discerned by revelation, "This one is mine." He did not select her because of her body. He identified her because of her origin. He said, "This one came out of me. This one carries my assignment. This one walks in my rhythm. This one can build with me."

That is unity at the root. Unity begins when you can look at one another and say, "We are not competitors. We are not strangers. We are not two separate brands trying to outshine each other. We are one expression of one assignment, given by one God, for one purpose." When a couple sees each other that way, arguments stop being wars and start becoming strategy meetings. Disagreements stop being personal attacks and start becoming calibration. The question is no longer, "Who's right?" The question becomes, "What protects the assignment God gave us?"

Unity is not sameness. Unity is agreement on direction. We may not always agree on every detail. We may not always like how the other person expressed a thought, handled a moment, or reacted in an emotional space. But disagreement does not have to mean division. Division literally means two visions, two directions, and two agendas. A house divided cannot stand because a house divided is not going anywhere together. But conflict, handled correctly, can actually strengthen unity. Conflict reveals where expectations were unspoken. Conflict reveals where motives were not yet purified. Conflict tells you, "Here is where we need to sit down, slow down, and hear God together."

Now, let's bring this into money, because this is where unity is tested and exposed most obviously. Money is one of the most spiritual things in your marriage, whether we like to admit that or not. Money will expose fear. It will expose control. It will expose insecurity. It will expose pride. It will expose resentment. It will expose whether you are partners or competitors. Money will tell you if you two are walking as one or quietly pulling apart.

Most couples are not financially cursed. They are financially divided. One is saving for stability while the other is spending for relief. One is tithing by faith while the other is withholding out of fear. One is planning for ownership and legacy while the other is simply surviving another week. One is silently resenting the other for "holding us back," while the other is silently resenting the one who "keeps trying to control." This is bigger than numbers. This is about being spirit-led. You cannot prosper in one bank account if you are spiritually living in two separate kingdoms.

Heaven funds unity. Heaven does not finance rebellion inside the covenant. God is not obligated to pour blessing into a divided structure. But when a man and woman present themselves before Him and say, "Father, this marriage is Yours. These finances are Yours. This vision is Yours. We come into agreement with Your will, not just our comfort," something supernatural begins to happen. Provision starts to respond to agreement.

This is why I say that marriage is heaven's business venture. You and your spouse are joint stewards of something that belongs to God. You are not just living together. You are governing together. The two of you have been entrusted with territory: spiritual, relational, generational, and financial territory. Your home is not just an address. Your home is an embassy. Your marriage is not just a relationship. Your marriage is an office. Your last name is not just sentimental. Your last name is a government.

Once you understand that, you stop treating money emotionally and start treating it prophetically. Money is not just for bills. Money is for assignment. Money is for positioning. Money is for building altars in the earth: altars called businesses, altars called homes, and altars called scholarships for your children and for children who do not carry your last name but carry your heart. Money is not supposed to be your god, but it is supposed to be your tool. It is meant to be placed, aimed, and released on purpose. And when a husband and wife agree on purpose, money finally has instruction.

Many couples are praying for more income while refusing to come into agreement. They are asking God to bless what they have not yet submitted. Hear me with love: God does not multiply what you hide. Unity invites increase because unity signals stewardship. When we agree, we become safe for God to trust. We become reliable enough for God to fund. We become mature enough to receive provision without worshiping it or turning it into a weapon against each other.

This is why the enemy attacks unity. He is not just trying to make you argue. He is trying to break your economic authority. He is trying to stop the assignment. He knows that if you ever truly sit down together, husband, wife, and Holy Spirit, and say, “This is our direction, this is our discipline, this is our standard, this is our covenant, this is how we sow, this is how we save, this is how we build, this is how we protect what God is giving us,” then something dangerous happens to darkness. You become predictable in righteousness. You become reliable in obedience. And a reliable marriage is a wealthy marriage because heaven will always resource what heaven can trust.

Now I want to speak gently to the matter of love, because love itself must be redefined in our homes. Our culture has trained us to love by reason: “I love her because she supports me.” “I love him because he provides.” “I love her because she’s beautiful.” “I love him because he makes me feel safe.” There is nothing wrong with appreciating those qualities, but if you make them the reason for your love, you have already built instability into your covenant.

Because what happens in seasons where she is exhausted and has nothing left to pour? What happens in seasons where he is broken and can't "be strong" for a moment? What happens when there is grief, disappointment, loss of a parent, loss of a job, a diagnosis, a spiritual attack, or spiritual dryness?

If your love was built on what they do, your love will begin to dissolve when they can no longer do it. God never gave us a reason for His love. "For God so loved the world that He gave His only begotten Son." He loved, and so He gave. Love, in the Kingdom, is not a feeling. Love is an action. Love is evidence. Love is demonstrated. Love moves. Love sacrifices. Love covers. Love endures. Love corrects. Love restores. Love keeps showing up even when emotions are tired. If I am made in the image and likeness of God, then that is the standard of love I am called to reflect in my marriage. Simply put, I love because I am a representation of love, and I have decided to give it to you. I love you, and I choose to build. I love you, and I choose to pray for you when you can't pray for yourself. I love you, and I choose to stay submitted to God so that I don't poison this home with my own ego.

That kind of love stabilizes vision. That kind of love stabilizes money. Because when we are rooted in unconditional love, fear loses its leverage. Control loses its leverage. Manipulation loses its leverage. We are not bargaining with love; we are ministering love. Hear me: marriage is ministry. Your tone toward your spouse is ministry. Your patience is ministry. Your honesty is ministry.

Your humility when you are wrong is ministry. Your consistency with money is ministry. Your refusal to hide spending is ministry. Your willingness to ask, "Are you okay?" instead of assuming, is ministry. Your home is the first pulpit God ever gave you. And if ministry is happening properly inside the home, there will be fruit. That fruit looks like peace. That fruit looks like clarity. That fruit looks like financial stability, even in uncertain seasons. That fruit looks like children who feel covered, not just disciplined. That fruit looks like the presence of God being consistent in your living room, not just in your church.

Unity produces fruit. Division produces performance. A divided couple can look "strong" in public and be dying in private. A united couple can look quiet in public and be shaking realms in private. Never envy what you see from the outside. The true test of unity is not social media. The true test of unity is atmosphere. Does the presence of God rest in this house? Can you feel peace when you walk in the door? Do you and your spouse know how to return to each other after a disagreement? Do you both feel safe enough to tell the truth without being punished for it? Safety is evidence of unity.

Now, what if unity is not present? What if you are reading this and saying, "We love each other, but we are not on the same page. We are spiritually out of rhythm, emotionally distant, financially divided. We've hurt each other. We've said things we can't take back. We don't even talk about money unless we're arguing."

Then I want to tell you something in love: unity can be rebuilt. But the first step is humility before God. Unity does not begin with, "You need to change." Unity begins with, "Father, change me." True unity is impossible without personal surrender. We must individually repent for the pride, the fear, the secrecy, the unforgiveness, the comparison, the silent punishments, and the financial manipulation. We must name it, not justify it, but name it. "Lord, I confess the ways I have tried to control instead of trust. I confess the ways I have spent without agreement. I confess the ways I have loved conditionally. I confess the words I have spoken that tore down my own home. Forgive me."

After repentance comes conversation. Real conversation. Not accusation disguised as conversation. Not interrogation disguised as concern. Honest conversation, with a new rule in place: in this conversation, we are not enemies. We are not prosecuting each other. We are not trying to win. We are not building a case. We are not looking for ammunition to use later. We are looking for clarity, because clarity is the foundation for unity.

Then comes vision. You must return to the question: "Why did God put us together?" Not "Why did we choose each other?" but "Why did God join us?" The first question measures preference. The second measures purpose. When you rediscover purpose, you rediscover partnership. You begin to remember, "We were not random. We were assigned."

And from there flows financial redirection. People underestimate how spiritual it is to sit down together and say,

"This is what comes into this house. This is how we will honor God with it. This is what we will not spend on. This is what we are saving toward. This is what we are building. This is what we are sowing into. This is the business we are birthing. This is the debt we are destroying. This is the inheritance we are creating for our children and our children's children." That is worship. That is spiritual maturity. That is spiritual warfare. That is unity made visible.

You cannot be "one flesh" and live two financial lives, not if you want power, not if you want peace, and not if you want your house to be trusted with true increase. Covenant demands agreement. Agreement activates authority.

I want to leave you with this: when a husband and wife walk together in unity, spiritually submitted to God, emotionally humble toward each other, and financially aligned in purpose, they begin to carry a sound. Heaven hears that sound. Hell fears that sound. Their children inherit that sound. Their resources start obeying that sound. That sound is called order. Unity is holy order. And holy order is the birthplace of holy wealth.

So this is my prayer for you, for your home, for your name: May unity be restored where it has been fractured. May identity be discovered where it was never taught. May love mature beyond conditions. May conversation replace accusation. May agreement replace silent war. May money become an instrument of purpose and not a source of torment. May your marriage take its rightful place, not as a performance for people, but as an instrument of God.

Father, we submit this marriage to You. We submit our vision, our choices, our money, our habits, our fears, our timelines, our expectations, and our disappointments. Teach us to move as one. Teach us to love like You, without condition, without expiration, without fear. Teach us to handle what You've given us with reverence. Let this covenant be trustworthy to heaven. Let this home become an embassy of Your presence. Let our unity become the ground where future generations learn what love, order, wealth, and holiness look like when they live together in the same house. In Jesus' name, Amen.

Lolita Brown

Every strong financial house begins long before money ever enters the picture. It begins before the paycheck, before the investment, before the savings plan, even before the first budget meeting. True prosperity begins with one word: agreement.

Most couples assume their financial future will be determined by their income, their discipline, their budgeting habits, or their ability to avoid debt. While these things matter, they are not the foundation. The real success of a marriage, in love or in money, always begins with unity.

Scripture asks a powerful question:

"How can two walk together unless they agree?" (Amos 3:3)

Agreement isn't about thinking the same thoughts every moment. It is about walking in the same direction. Agreement is alignment, spiritually, emotionally, and purposefully. It is two hearts postured toward the same future, even if they arrive at that vision for different reasons.

Unity is the currency of heaven. And when a husband and wife are unified, everything else becomes easier: communication, planning, decision-making, building, saving, investing, giving, and even dreaming. But when unity breaks down, the finances break with it.

I've sat across from couples who were brilliant, capable, successful people, yet struggling financially, not because they lacked money, but because they lacked agreement. Once unity is restored, blessings flow where frustration once lived.

Let me show you what I mean.

One Couple, One House, Two Visions—Until Unity Arrived

Years ago, I worked with a couple who desperately wanted to buy a home. The husband saw the house as stability, a place to anchor their future. His wife saw it as legacy, something they could build and eventually pass down to their children. They were fighting for the same blessing, but they were fighting each other instead of the problem. He thought she was dragging her feet. She thought he was rushing the process. He saw her caution as doubt. She saw his zeal as pressure. But when we finally paused and peeled back the layers, what surfaced was beautiful:

They both wanted the same dream. They had simply never articulated why. When they finally sat down, expressed their hearts to one another, and heard each other's values, fears, dreams, and motives, something powerful happened. The disagreement softened. Understanding entered. And unity emerged.

Once they prayed together about timing, their vision became one vision. Once they aligned their hearts, wisdom took the lead. Suddenly, the home-buying process felt guided, not forced. And within weeks, the exact home they needed presented itself. What striving couldn't accomplish, unity attracted effortlessly.

Prosperity Begins in the Heart, Not the Wallet

Money is spiritual and practical. Money reveals how we see the world. This is why unity matters so deeply. A couple may fight about overspending, saving, budgeting, or debt, but beneath the surface, the real conflict is usually about something deeper:

One spouse sees money as protection because they grew up in lack. The other sees money as freedom because they grew up under restriction. One feels safe when the account is full. The other feels alive when opportunities flow. One plans every detail. The other just wants peace. Neither posture is wrong. Neither desire is immoral. Neither style is superior. They are simply different. And if these differences are not understood, honored, and harmonized, they turn into division. And division always blocks multiplication.

But when two people learn to understand each other and begin seeing each other not as the problem, but as partners with different strengths, this is the beginning of wealth. Unity does not mean sameness; it means harmony. Two different notes creating a stronger sound. Financial unity is less about money and more about merging values, experiences, and expectations into a shared vision.

Love First, Strategy Second

Couples often come to me expecting strategies, budgets, plans, systems, tools, and timelines. And while those things absolutely matter, none of them will work in a house divided. If love is not the foundation, money will become a battleground. I remind couples of this every day:

Money is a tool, not a test.

A blessing, not a battleground.

A resource, not a ruler.

When love leads, financial fear loses its power.

When humility enters, pride has no room to sabotage.

When unity becomes the goal, money becomes simple again.

But unity requires intention.

It requires vulnerability.

It requires communication.

And above all, it requires God.

Because unity is not a human achievement, it is a spiritual one.

The Prayer That Changes Everything

There have been many moments in my own marriage where my husband and I stood at opposite ends of a major decision, seasons where I carried the plan and he carried the passion, and both were necessary, yet not yet aligned.

I remember one moment in particular. We were considering a large investment. My heart said yes. His spirit said not yet. And for a moment, it felt like we were speaking two different languages.

Instead of pushing toward a win, we paused, joined hands, quieted our emotions, and invited God into the conversation. Within twenty-four hours, clarity came, and it was unmistakable and undeniable. The opportunity revealed itself, and peace followed like a river. Prayer bridged the gap where conversation struggled, broke the tension that logic could not break, and created a unity that strategy alone could never provide.

Jesus said: *"Where two or three are gathered in My name, there I am in the midst of them."* (*Matthew 18:20*)

When couples pray together, they stop battling each other and start partnering with heaven. They stop wrestling in their own strength and begin receiving divine guidance. They stop seeing their spouse as the obstacle and begin seeing God as the source. Unity becomes easy when God is at the center of it.

When a Marriage Walks as One, Heaven Moves Swiftly

Unity is a force, an expression of favor and a form of spiritual intelligence. When a couple walks in true oneness, everything accelerates: opportunities open more quickly, provision comes with greater ease, wisdom becomes clearer, fear loses its grip, peace fills the home, and decisions become guided rather than pressured. Unity multiplies every blessing and minimizes every burden, while division delays destiny. Agreement, however, has the power to propel a marriage forward with supernatural momentum.

And I have seen this not only spiritually, but practically. The couples who thrive financially are not always the ones who make the most money. They are the ones who honor each other's voice, value each other's gifts, pray together, and refuse to see each other as opponents.

They understand that money is not "yours" or "mine." It is ours, entrusted to us by God for a divine mission. Marriage is not two people running two separate races. Marriage is two people running one race with two sets of strengths.

When you become unified in purpose, strategy, and prayer, you unlock an entirely new currency, one heaven recognizes and multiplies. If there is one message I could tattoo on the heart of every married couple, it is this: Unity is your greatest financial strategy. Not hustle. Not saving. Not budgeting. Not investing. Not even income. Unity.

When two people agree fully, willingly, and spiritually, there is no limit to what God can release into their hands. Two visions merge into one. Two strengths become one force. And two prayers rise as one sound in the ears of heaven. Once unity is established, the possibilities become endless. When you and your spouse walk together, truly together, there are no ceilings, no enemies strong enough, no obstacle too large, and no financial mountain immovable. Unity is more than agreement; it is an anointing, and it remains the greatest wealth-builder of all.

Reflection Questions

1. Take a moment to honestly reflect, together or individually, on the state of unity in your financial life:

____

____

____

____

2. Which money conversations tend to create the most tension between us?

____

____

____

____

____

3. Where do our financial goals align, and where do they differ?

____

____

____

____

____

4. Do we truly understand each other's values, fears, and motivations around money?

____

____

____

____

5. How often do we pause to pray before making financial decisions?

____

____

____

____

6. What new systems or habits could help us communicate better and celebrate our progress more intentionally?

____

____

____

____

Action Steps

Put unity into practice with simple, intentional steps:

1. Pray daily for unity, inviting God to align your hearts and guide your decisions.
2. Write your couple's mission statement, clarifying the purpose behind your financial life together.
3. Schedule your first money meeting, and speak faith over your finances out loud as a united team.
4. Revisit your goals monthly, tracking both your numbers and your oneness as you build a future anchored in agreement.

Chapter Five

WALKING IN FAITH - HOW PURPOSE DRIVES WEALTH

Wealth is not the goal. Wealth is not the reward. Wealth is not the dream. Wealth is the result. When a person begins to walk in the purpose God designed for them, provision begins to respond. Doors begin to appear where there were none. Resources begin to gather. People begin to find you. Wisdom begins to increase. Opportunities start calling you by name. Why? Because in the Kingdom, wealth is not something you chase. Wealth is something that answers you.

We have been taught by culture, by parents, by school systems, and by fear to chase money. We were trained, almost without thinking, to submit to an earthly system that tells us the pathway to security looks like this: You go to school, you get good grades, you go to college, you pick a respectable career, you get hired, you climb, you save, and you retire. Or, in another version of the same approach, you become an entrepreneur because someone in your family owned a business and brought you in early. You were given a shortcut. The door that most people would have had to knock on for a decade, you were quietly brought through the back of. And that is what many cultures around the world call success.

In many households, whether we are talking about the United States, the Caribbean, India, West Africa, or East Asia, it is understood that success means becoming a doctor, a lawyer, an engineer, a dentist, or something else with a title that produces money and status. Some of us grew up with that quiet pressure: Make the family proud by becoming something profitable.

Now, I am not attacking those fields. They are honorable. They are needed. They are often high-demand, high-income, respected professions. But I want you to hear me very clearly: A career is not automatically a calling. An income stream is not automatically an assignment. A respected job title is not automatically destiny.

The danger is that we confuse pathway with purpose. We assume because something looks stable, it must be God. We assume because something pays well, it must be right. We assume because a position is admired, it must be honorable in heaven. But purpose is not a salary. Purpose is not applause. Purpose is not safety. Purpose is the reason God sent you here.

Every one of us was born as an answer. That is what purpose is. Purpose is the specific problem in the earth that your life was designed to solve. It is the area of life that stirs you, burdens you, irritates you, convicts you, moves you, and will not leave you alone. Purpose is the assignment God stamped onto your soul before you were ever given a name.

This is why purpose and wealth are spiritually connected. Because if wealth comes from purpose, and purpose comes from God, then real wealth is grace and mercy from God, along with the privilege and blessing of walking with Him. This is what I mean when I say "walking in faith." Faith is not just believing God will do something for you. Faith is agreeing to do what God sent you here to do, even when it does not look profitable yet. Faith is saying yes to purpose before the paycheck shows up. Faith trusts that whatever God orders, He also funds. We do not live like that because it was very seldom modeled for us.

From the time we were children, most of us were taught how to function in the world, not how to function within ourselves. We were taught how to be polite, how to greet people, how to respect our teachers, and how to behave in public. Some of us were raised in homes where manners were everything, where you could not walk into a room without saying, "Good morning," where not greeting someone was considered disrespectful. We were taught how to make sure everyone else felt honored.

But very few of us were ever taught how to honor ourselves. We were not taught, "Sit with God and ask Him who you are." We were not taught, "Go to your room, close the door, and ask the Lord, 'What did You put me here to do?'" We were not trained to study our own heart, our own burdens, our own wiring, or our own calling. We were taught how to coexist with others, but not how to be in covenant with purpose.

That is one of the main reasons so many full-grown adults wake up every morning frustrated. You have people who are technically successful, with good jobs, decent homes, reliable cars, benefits, savings accounts, and still they are not at peace. Still they are restless. Still they are irritated on Monday mornings. Still they go to bed with a heaviness they cannot name. Why? Because they are living produced lives, not purposed lives.

Produced life: A life built by expectation.

Purposed life: A life built by assignment.

A produced life sounds like, "This is what your father did, so this is what you will do," or, "This is the stable path, go do this," or, "This is what everyone in this family becomes." A produced life is often celebrated publicly and suffocating privately. You are getting applause for playing a role you were never born to carry.

A purposed life is different. It often begins in discomfort. It often begins with something that bothers you so deeply that you cannot walk away from it. That is usually your first clue. That thing that disturbs you, frustrates you, or moves you to tears is often the doorway to your calling.

For me, I'll tell you plainly: It was relationships. I did not understand it at the time, and for years I thought it was actually my weakness. I noticed from a very young age that broken relationships grieved me in a way they didn't seem to grieve other people. When my parents weren't in harmony, I felt it like a physical ache. When I saw my brothers and sisters not getting along, it hit me heavily. When I watched my sisters in pain, trying to survive heartbreak, trying to hold themselves together, I carried that. I couldn't shake it. I would replay conversations. I would internalize their sadness. I would sit with their questions as though they were my own.

And because of the way we train boys to be tough, don't feel, don't show softness, don't "act sensitive," I thought something was wrong with me. I thought I needed to harden up. I thought I needed to numb that tenderness in me because it didn't match what "manhood" was supposed to look like.

But what I thought was weakness was actually assignment. That grief was not weakness. That grief was God pointing at my calling. It was heaven whispering, "You're called to heal this."

In Scripture, we see this over and over. Moses was not moved into destiny by comfort. He was moved by anger. He could not stomach seeing his people oppressed. He couldn't watch injustice and stay calm. That anger pushed him into a confrontation that ultimately became messy, but it also revealed his assignment: deliverer.

Purpose often announces itself first as agitation. Think about that. The thing you "can't stand" may be the very thing you are here to stand in the middle of. The thing that irritates you deeply, "Why do families keep falling apart like this?" "Why are kids growing up without fathers?" "Why is the healthcare system like this?" "Why is education like this?" "Why are our communities built like this?" may be God pointing at your lane.

When you see that, stop running from it. Lean into it. That is the place where grace flows. And where grace flows, supply flows. Provision is tied to assignment. Provision responds to purpose. If you are operating in what God sent you to the earth to do, heaven is obligated to fund you. You are not some random volunteer doing God a favor. You are an ambassador on assignment. The Kingdom takes care of its ambassadors.

This is why I say: Wealth is a byproduct of purpose. Wealth is the fruit of obedience. If you're exhausted from chasing money, that exhaustion is telling you something. It's telling you, "You are sourcing yourself from the wrong system."

There are two systems at play: the world's system and the Kingdom system. The world's system is built around self-preservation. It says, "Protect yourself, advance yourself, secure yourself, promote yourself." It tells you your value is determined by your usefulness to an employer or a market. It trains you to fear not having enough. Scarcity is its language. Anxiety is its fuel.

The Kingdom system is different. The Kingdom system is not a democracy. You don't vote God in and out. He is King. His Word is final. His design is intentional. His order is perfect. His provision is guaranteed, but only under His order. The Kingdom system is built around assignment. The question in the Kingdom is not, "How much can you get?" The question is, "What were you sent to do?" Because once we answer that, the rest begins to arrange itself.

This is why Genesis is so precious to me. In Genesis 1, God reveals how life was meant to function: "Let us make man in Our image, after Our likeness, and let them have dominion." He is revealing the original contract. "I am making you in My image." That is identity. "I am giving you My likeness." That is personality and function. "I am giving you dominion." That is authority, rulership, stewardship, and responsibility. Dominion means rulership. It means governing a territory. You are here to govern something.

But how can I govern if I don't know what I've been assigned to govern? How can I take dominion if I don't even know my lane? This is why so many of us feel powerless. We keep trying to apply dominion to areas we were never assigned to rule. We're trying to enter industries we were never called to influence. We're trying to impress people we were never called to serve. We're trying to imitate lives we were never designed to live. And the result is unfullfilment and loneliness.

That is not God's will for you.

Hear me: you were not created to spend the majority of your waking hours doing something that depletes you just so you can afford a life you don't even have time to enjoy. That is not dominion. That is slavery dressed in professionalism.

Now, let me be balanced. I am not saying, "Leave your job tomorrow." I am not saying, "Walk away from responsibility." Purpose is not recklessness. Purpose is order. Purpose is stewardship. Purpose is clarity. Sometimes, yes, your job is the assignment. God absolutely places people in medicine, law, politics, tech, art, construction, logistics, education, finance, and engineering.

Sometimes your career and your calling are the same stream. Sometimes they are not. Sometimes the job is a classroom. Sometimes the job is provision for a season while God develops what you're truly called to do. Sometimes the job is exposure; you're meeting people you will one day serve. Sometimes the job is a training ground; you are learning systems and language that you will one day redeem for the Kingdom.

So I am not telling you to walk out. I am asking you: Do you know why you're there? If you don't know why you are where you are, you are in danger of wasting the season you're in. Purpose gives meaning to seasons that don't feel glamorous. When you know that you are assigned, even if you are not yet in your dream lane, you can endure with joy. Joy, not just tolerance. Joy.

Happiness depends on circumstances lining up the way you prefer. Joy flows from alignment, even under pressure. Joy says, "I know God is using this." Joy says, "This is connected to something larger." Joy says, "There is oil on this. I am being shaped to carry what I asked God to trust me with."

That is why you must pursue clarity about your purpose, not for ego, but for order. Not so you can brand yourself, but so you can govern yourself. Because when you finally know the reason you are here, two powerful things happen.

First, you begin to release the need for constant approval from others. The need for social media applause diminishes. The need for your family to finally say, "We're proud of you," begins to loosen. You become rooted. You become internally fed. You become anchored in this truth: "God sent me here for this. I am not random." That is spiritual maturity.

Second, your life becomes disciplined, not because someone is forcing you, and not because you are afraid of consequences, but because you are too focused to waste yourself. Purpose is the greatest form of self-control. When you have purpose, you no longer need rules to control you from the outside; conviction begins to govern you from the inside.

"I don't talk like that. I don't move like that. I don't spend like that. I don't give myself to that. I don't go there. I don't attach myself to that situation. Why? Because I know why I'm here, and that does not serve why I'm here." That is holy discipline. And that discipline is the soil wealth grows in.

Now I want to talk to parents and future parents for a moment. We must do what some of our parents were not equipped to do for us. We must raise children in honor and order, yes. Respect your elders, yes. Speak well, yes. But we must go further. We must teach our sons and daughters how to be right within themselves and in covenant with the Father.

We must sit them down and ask:

"What moves you?"

"What do you dream about when no one is telling you what to dream?"

"What do you see that bothers you so deeply you can't ignore it?"

"What do you feel responsible for, even though you seem too young for that kind of responsibility?"

"What do you love so much that time disappears when you're doing it?"

And then we must tell them: "God loves you. God is going to use you mightily. God did not place you here randomly. You are an answer to something in the earth."

Why? Because if we don't give them identity, a sense of God-ordained self, the world will gladly sell them identity. And identity for sale always comes with chains.

This is not self-help. These are spiritual words. When Jesus was asked, "What is the greatest commandment?" He answered, *"Love the Lord your God with all your heart, all your soul, all your mind, and all your strength."* Then He said something that many of us quote but do not fully hear: "And love your neighbor as yourself." We love that part, "love your neighbor." We preach that part. We demand that part. Be kind. Be respectful. Treat people well. Be generous. Be forgiving. Yes, all of that is true. But notice: Jesus set a condition. "Love your neighbor as yourself."

You cannot love your neighbor if you despise yourself. You cannot pour into your marriage if you are empty within. You cannot raise children in stability when you secretly hate your own reflection. You cannot serve with purity if the only reason you're serving is to feel valuable for five minutes. To love your neighbor well, you must first be at peace with who you are. And you cannot be at peace with who you are until you know why you are.

Purpose is not selfish. Purpose is stewardship of self so that you can be poured out rightly. And this is where wealth returns to the conversation. When you begin to live in purpose, you become a source of impact. You start solving problems in the earth. You start meeting needs. You start answering prayers. You start filling gaps. You start healing patterns. And when you do that, people begin to honor what you carry. Doors open. Resources move. Favor gathers. Influence builds. Income follows. Wealth is drawn to solutions.

The Bible says, "Your gift will make room for you." Not your job. Not your résumé. Your gift. The thing God placed in you that solves a problem on this earth. When you begin to use that faithfully, consistently, and obediently, that gift becomes a key. It unlocks rooms you could not have accessed by networking alone. It puts you in front of people you normally would never meet. It qualifies you in spaces where you are, on paper, "unqualified." That access is provision. That access is wealth formation. That access is legacy infrastructure.

And I need you to hear this: God will do it in a way that brings Him glory, not your glory. Sometimes He will allow people to underestimate you, overlook you, and even mistreat you because all of that becomes part of the testimony. Joseph's brothers sold him because they envied him. They thought they were removing him from his rightful place with his father. They did not realize they were transporting him into position. Joseph went from the pit, to slavery, to prison, to palace. And what looked like betrayal was actually placement. By the time famine hit, Joseph was not just saving himself; he was feeding nations. That is what purpose does. Purpose is bigger than you. Purpose feeds nations.

And that is why wealth in the Kingdom is never selfish. Wealth is not, "Look what I have." Wealth is, "Look what I can now build, fund, protect, heal, restore, and release." Wealth is a tool to accomplish assignment. Wealth is meant to finance impact.

So I will ask you directly: The dream you are chasing, who does it bless? If the fullness of your dream came true tomorrow, would only you and your household benefit, or would people outside your last name be lifted because of it? Because God is not obligated to fund personal projects. But He will pour unlimited resources into a life that is dedicated to solving the burdens on His heart.

God has burdens. God has concerns in the earth. God has areas that grieve Him. And those burdens are where He plants people. So when you feel pulled toward or grieved over a certain issue, do not brush that off as, "Oh, I'm emotional." Ask, "Lord, is this one of Your burdens? Are You calling me into this? Is this where my wealth is supposed to flow?"

Purpose protects money from becoming an idol. Purpose tells money where to go. Money without purpose will rule you. Money under purpose will serve you. That's why you have people who make more money than they've ever made and are more miserable than they've ever been. Money magnifies what's already there. If all that's in you is emptiness, then more money will give you the ability to express that emptiness louder, faster, and on a larger scale. But if what's in you is assignment, then more money simply means more impact.

I want to invite you into practice now. This is where walking in faith becomes practical, not just poetic. If you are married, I want you and your spouse to walk through this exercise together, but I want each of you to take some time to do it individually first. If you are single, do it yourself before the Lord. At night, when the house is quiet, after the kids are asleep if you have children, and after the noise of the day has settled, sit in stillness. No TV. No distractions. No music unless it is worship that keeps you focused. Keep the lights low. And I want you to say, out loud:

"Father, I thank You for the gift of life. I thank You that Your DNA runs through me. I repent for every place I have lived by the world's system instead of Your order. I repent for choosing survival over obedience. I repent for living for applause. I repent for ignoring the burden You placed in me. Show me why You sent me here. Reveal my assignment. I don't want to spend another year out of position. I surrender."

Then be quiet.

Your mind may wander at first. That's normal. Bring it back by praying Scripture. One of my favorites is, "Many are the plans in a man's heart, but the Lord's purpose will prevail." I personalize it: "Many are the plans in my heart, but Lord, let Your purpose prevail in my life." Say it slowly. Let it settle. Repeat it until your soul calms down and your mind stops chasing noise. Stay there for twenty minutes, or thirty if you can. You may not hear anything dramatic the first time, and that's all right.

Often, what will happen is that God will begin to visit you in your dreams that same night. He will begin to replay images, situations, ideas, people, and burdens. He will begin to point. He will begin to highlight. Write it down in the morning. Do this again and again. You are training your spirit to listen. You are training your life to submit. You are training your will to bow.

Then, and this part matters, come together with your spouse if you are married. Share what you sensed, even if you feel unsure. Compare notes. You may be surprised to find that God is speaking to both of you in alignment. Sometimes the confirmation is not in what you heard yourself, but in what your spouse heard and had no way of knowing you were receiving. This is how households come into divine order. This is how direction begins to crystallize. This is how unity is born around assignment.

And after prayer, after revelation, and after clarity begins, even if it is still in seed form, you must seek mentorship. We have lost this in the Church. The world uses mentorship ruthlessly. In entertainment, sports, finance, and politics, people are groomed, trained, and accelerated by those ahead of them. But in the Church, too many believers try to build alone. We romanticize isolation. We reject correction. We get offended by instruction. We call accountability "judgment." And we delay our own progress by ten or twenty years because we refuse to sit at the feet of someone who is already carrying what we say we want.

Pride is expensive.

Find someone who is already walking in their purpose with fruit. Fruit means people are blessed and changed by their gifts. There is evidence of service to others, not self-promotion. Submit yourself to learn. Ask questions. Let them challenge you. Let them tell you what you do not want to hear. Let them show you how to build with wisdom so you do not have to keep starting over.

This is not weakness. This is Kingdom protocol. We are a body. No body part functions in isolation and survives. As you begin to walk in this, with clarity of purpose, discipline of life, unity in marriage, and humility in mentorship, you will notice something: Provision starts to appear. It may not come as a lottery moment. It may not come as a dramatic windfall. Often, it comes as a door: an invitation, a contract, a partnership, a room you are suddenly brought into, a conversation someone recommends you for, or an opportunity that should not have been yours, but somehow is. That is wealth beginning to answer you.

And when it does, remember this: The money is not for flexing. The money is not for ego. The money is not for revenge against the people who did not believe in you. The money is not so you can finally prove something to your old classmates, your ex, or your parents. That is limited thinking. That is still the world's system. In the Kingdom, money has a mission. Ask the Lord, "Where does this belong?" Because every dollar that comes into your life is either seed or strategy. Spend it like purpose, not like pain.

You are not called to live by the world's formula: running, hustling, grinding yourself to the bone, stressed, angry, spiritually empty, emotionally numb, financially scared, and pretending to be happy in pictures. You are called to live by Kingdom order. You are called to live by assignment. You are called to live by revelation. You are called to live by faith.

Faith is not superstition. Faith is structure. Faith is obedience. Faith is clarity. Faith is saying, "God, I align with Your purpose for my life, and I trust that as I walk in it, You will release everything required to fulfill it."

So hear me, and hear me with love: Stop chasing money. Chase God. Chase clarity. Chase assignment. Chase healing. Chase obedience. When you do that, money will start chasing you. And not just money, but wealth. The kind of wealth that builds homes for families who had none. The kind of wealth that funds scholarships. The kind of wealth that launches community centers. The kind of wealth that quietly pays another family's medical bill. The kind of wealth that creates ownership in neighborhoods that always seemed out of your reach. The kind of wealth that will outlive you. That is Kingdom wealth. That is what purpose attracts. That is what faith walks into.

I want you to understand something deep in your spirit: You are not behind. You are not late. You are not disqualified. You are not too old. You are not too damaged. You are not too uneducated. You are not too underexposed. You are not too inexperienced. You are not average. You are not just getting by. The fact that you are still breathing means assignment is still active. The fact that you can still feel that holy irritation in your chest when you see certain things means God is still pointing. The fact that you are reading these words means heaven is still recruiting you for what you were always meant to do.

Walk in faith. Discover your purpose. Submit to God's order. And watch wealth answer you, not as your master, but as your servant.

Lolita Brown

There comes a moment in every marriage when the chase for "more" begins to feel strangely hollow. More income. More credentials. More security. More accolades. Each of these pursuits has its place, yet without purpose directing them, they can begin to lose meaning. I've watched couples accumulate impressive salaries and still feel drained, defeated, and disconnected from one another. What they were missing wasn't money. It was assignment.

Purpose is the compass that steadies the heart and directs the household. It's what turns wealth from something you pursue with force into something you step into with grace. Purpose removes the frantic energy from the financial journey and replaces it with intentionality and peace.

As a wealth advisor, I've sat with countless couples who are intelligent, educated, and high-performing, yet financially exhausted. They weren't struggling because they were irresponsible or incapable. They were struggling because they were trying to build wealth before discovering why God had called them to build it in the first place. When purpose is absent, money becomes reactive. When purpose is present, money becomes strategic.

Purpose shapes how a couple sees their future. It gives clarity to their commitments, structure to their spending, and dignity to their discipline. And the beautiful truth is this: God never gives purpose without providing the resources to fulfill it. Provision flows wherever obedience leads.

When a husband and wife embrace the assignment placed on their marriage, their financial life takes on a new posture. They are no longer fighting for increase; they are aligning with it. They begin to make decisions rooted not in pressure, but in calling. They don't give because they fear lack; they give because they recognize abundance. They don't invest because someone told them to; they invest because they see the generational picture God is painting through their union. Purpose doesn't just point you toward wealth; it prepares you to sustain it.

Purpose Positions Couples for Provision

One of the most profound realities I've observed is how purpose tends to attract the very opportunities couples once felt they had to chase. Purpose has its own gravitational pull. When a couple steps into what God has instructed, resources begin to align almost effortlessly: ideas, relationships, open doors, divine connections. Not because they manipulated outcomes, but because they were already walking the path God paved for them.

So many households exhaust themselves trying to create opportunities, only to discover that the moment they embraced alignment, the opportunities began coming to them. Purpose has a way of quieting fear, sharpening vision, and strengthening resolve. It instills a confidence in couples that does not come from numbers on a bank statement, but from knowing they are walking in what heaven has authored.

When purpose is clear, planning becomes easier. Navigating slow seasons becomes less intimidating. Emotional giving evolves into structured stewardship. Creativity flourishes, and couples begin to see avenues for income and impact they had never considered before. And suddenly, what once felt impossible becomes not only reachable, but sustainable.

This is precisely why the enemy doesn't start by attacking finances. He starts by attacking identity and purpose. A couple disconnected from their assignment will always struggle to steward their provision. But a couple grounded in who they are, and confident in what God has called them to do, cannot be easily shaken.

Kingdom Wealth: A Higher Calling

As couples align with purpose, they begin to recognize the difference between worldly wealth and kingdom wealth. Worldly wealth is survival-driven. It is protective, possessive, and often rooted in fear. But kingdom wealth is purpose-driven, generous, expansive, and transformational.

Kingdom wealth doesn't just bless the couple; it blesses those connected to them. It lifts burdens. It funds visions. It creates opportunities. It becomes a conduit for change that echoes through communities and generations.

One of the defining characteristics of kingdom wealth is its intentionality. Money is not seen as a symbol of status, but as an instrument of assignment. It becomes a ministry in itself, an expression of obedience and partnership with God's will. A couple walking in purpose understands that wealth is not just something they accumulate; it is something they steward. Their giving becomes a lifestyle, not an emotional reaction. Their investments become a responsibility, not a gamble. Their financial planning becomes an act of worship.

When couples embrace this mindset, money becomes peaceful. It stops fighting against the marriage and begins working for it.

Purpose in Scripture: Wealth Followed Assignment

If you look closely at Scripture, you will notice a consistent pattern: God never released wealth without also releasing responsibility. Every individual or couple who walked in abundance did so because they were first walking in purpose.

The Proverbs 31 woman did not pursue wealth; she pursued excellence. She showed up in her gifts with consistency, integrity, and wisdom. Her increase was the natural fruit of a life aligned with purpose. Her household flourished because she flourished. Her business expanded because her diligence expanded. She didn't chase prosperity; she cultivated it.

Aquila and Priscilla are an example of marital purpose in motion. Their business was not separate from their ministry; it funded it. Their home became a place of teaching, equipping, and hosting. Their assignment brought favor to their business, and their business made room for their assignment.

Abraham and Sarah walked in obedience, even when the instructions seemed illogical. Their wealth became the visible expression of God's covenant with them. Joseph, through integrity and unwavering commitment to purpose, was positioned to manage the wealth of a nation and preserve the life of his own family.

Scripture teaches us this one truth: God funds what He ordains. Whatever vision God gives a marriage, He also gives the provision, often in seed form, requiring stewardship, discipline, unity, and faith to cultivate it.

Aligning Your Wealth With Your Assignment

Every marriage has a unique purpose. Some are called to build businesses, others to build communities, others to build families, ministries, or structures that strengthen future generations. Purpose is not one-size-fits-all, but it is always intentional.

When couples discover their shared assignment, their financial choices begin to make sense. They stop comparing themselves to other households. They stop following trends, fads, and pressure-driven expectations. They begin to make decisions that reflect destiny, not culture.

Wealth becomes personal. It becomes sacred. It becomes a reflection of identity and calling.

A couple committed to purpose begins praying before planning. They seek God for direction rather than asking Him to bless a direction they've already chosen. And because prayer becomes strategy, their financial foundation grows firm, even in unstable seasons.

Purpose brings order. And order invites increase.

Walking Boldly Into Purpose-Driven Wealth

Wealth is not random. It is not the result of wishing, hoping, or working ourselves into exhaustion. Wealth is the natural expression of alignment. When husband and wife walk confidently in their God-given assignment, grace flows. Favor increases. Doors open. Ideas multiply. The right people appear at the right time. The household begins to experience what can only be described as divine synchronicity: heaven backing their efforts, heaven blessing their unity, heaven honoring their obedience.

Your marriage is not simply building wealth; your marriage is constructing legacy. And legacy is never accidental. It is the result of purpose embraced, obedience practiced, stewardship refined, and faith exercised consistently.

Walk in faith.

Walk in purpose.

Walk in confidence.

And watch God release the wealth that has always been attached to your name.

Chapter Six

TRUSTING GOD DURING SETBACKS, OVERCOMING FINANCIAL CHALLENGES TOGETHER

Van Brown

One of the most damaging lies many believers quietly carry is this: "If I'm really walking with God, I won't go through hardship." That belief sounds comforting at first. It sounds like security. It sounds like favor. It makes us feel like we've finally found a way to guarantee safety. But it is not biblical. It is not true. And when we believe it, it sets us up for disappointment, offense toward God, and even division within our own home.

Scripture never promised us a life without trouble. In fact, the opposite is true. The Bible says, "When trouble comes," not "if trouble comes." When, not if. The language of God is honest. God does not flirt with us. He does not manipulate us into the Kingdom with false promises. He never said, "Follow Me and you will never cry again." He said, "Follow Me, and even when you cry, I will carry you through it." This means something we must understand if we are going to build spiritually strong marriages, spiritually strong families, and spiritually strong financial lives: challenges are not evidence that God left you. Many times, challenges are evidence that God is maturing you.

Every human being is born as a solution to something on the earth. You did not just show up. You were sent. You are not random. You are an answer. And if God sent you as an answer, then that means, by definition, He sent you to a place where there are problems. You cannot be trusted to carry solutions if you've never sat in need. You cannot speak deliverance with authority if you've never felt pressure. You cannot comfort others if you've never survived pain.

So the question is not, "Will I face trouble?" The question is, "When trouble visits my house, whose voice will I listen to?"

This is where the believer and the unbeliever begin to separate.

The world looks at a crisis and sees only the crisis. Bills are late, income dropped, an unexpected medical cost hit, the car got repossessed, a job ended, rent is behind, and the world says, "This is disaster. I'm alone in this. It's all on me. I have to fix this. I have to fix this now."

And so the weight of the crisis sits entirely on their shoulders. The crisis becomes the new god. The crisis becomes the thing they revolve everything around. The fear of the crisis begins speaking louder than hope, louder than peace, louder than wisdom, louder than truth. All of their decisions now flow from survival.

But the believer is called to live differently.

I did not say the believer will never feel panic. I did not say the believer will never feel fear. I did not say the believer will never feel pressure. We are subject to be led by our emotions. We have bodies. We have nervous systems. We have hearts. We have responsibilities. We are allowed to feel. But spiritually, in the Kingdom, we are taught something higher: even this is working for my good. Even this is being woven into a testimony. Even this is being used to shape me, mature me, elevate me, and position me. Even this will glorify God.

This is the quiet advantage of the children of God: not that we avoid the storm, but that we cannot be destroyed by it.

Jesus said, "In this world you will have many troubles. But be of good cheer, for I have overcome the world." That is not poetic language. That is legal language. That is covenant language. God is saying, "You're going to feel what everyone else feels. You're going to walk through what everyone else walks through. But you are not walking through it with the same covering. I have already overcome what you are about to face. You may be going through it for the first time. I am not. I already beat this."

And if we are in Him, if we truly belong to Him, then whatever He overcame, we now share in the victory of. That is the psychology of the Kingdom. That is the philosophy of the

Kingdom. That is the culture of the Kingdom. And that is why, in the Kingdom, peace is not based on circumstances. Peace is based on position.

Let's talk about that peace, because if we do not define it, we will keep chasing a false version of it.

Most of us have been conditioned to define peace as: "All my bills are paid, I have extra in the account, nothing is pressing me, and I don't feel threatened."

That is not spiritual peace. That is comfort.

Comfort is fragile. Comfort is easily stolen. Comfort is emotional quiet because everything is currently going your way. You can have comfort without faith.

Peace is different. Peace is authority. Peace is rooted in who you belong to, not what you currently have. Kingdom peace says, "Even if we are three months behind on rent right now, I refuse to let rent become my god. Even if they repossess the car tomorrow, I refuse to let a car become my identity. Even if my student loan notice just arrived in all caps, I will not trade my worship of God for worship of this debt. Even if I don't know how this medical bill will be paid, I will not let fear sit on the throne of my mind."

Whatever you obsess over becomes your god. If you obsess over the bill more than you magnify the Lord, the bill becomes your ruler. And I say this with compassion: those rulers are cruel. Debt is a cruel god. Scarcity is a cruel god. Financial fear is a cruel god. They will steal your sleep, break your health, drain your marriage, harden your tone with your children, and poison your mind. They will convince you that you are failing, when in truth you're just in training.

Setbacks are training.

Financial pressure is not always evidence of failure. Financial pressure is often evidence that God is allowing you to experience a classroom.

Think about it. If part of your future impact is helping other couples restore their homes, teaching young men how to build with integrity, helping single mothers stabilize their households, showing churches how to steward money properly, or leading teams through economic valleys, the credibility to speak into those areas cannot come from theory alone. You have to have some scars. You have to know what lack feels like, not just what abundance feels like. You have to know the emotions that come with, "We might have to move out." You may recognize the way your chest tightens when you check an account and it's not enough. You have to know those feelings so that when you tell somebody, "You're going to make it," they can feel that you're not guessing. Authority is born in affliction.

So what the world calls "embarrassing," heaven calls "credentialing."

Now, let's be honest about something that sits at the center of most marriages: money tension. Study after study will tell you that money is one of the leading causes of divorce. I believe that is only partially true. The deeper truth is this: it's not money itself. It's the way we communicate around money. Most couples have never been taught how to face crisis together without attacking each other.

When finances tighten, the house becomes a courtroom. Spouses become witnesses against one another. "You shouldn't have spent that." "I told you we shouldn't have moved here." "Why didn't you get a second job?" "Why didn't you listen to me?" "You're too relaxed." "You're too controlling." "You're too emotional." "You don't take this seriously." "You don't believe in me."

But when we turn on each other, we're doing the enemy's work for him. He doesn't even have to divide the house; we volunteer to do it ourselves. The two that God called to be one start standing on opposite sides of the table, like rivals, instead of shoulder to shoulder like partners. And remember what we said earlier in this book: Division means two visions. Once there are two visions in a crisis, the crisis wins.

So, we must learn a different response.

When a financial hit comes, instead of letting panic speak first, we have to let honor speak first. Instead of, "You failed," we need, "We are here together." Instead of, "Look what you did," we say, "Let us go to God together." This does not mean we ignore reality. It means we refuse to surrender to accusation. Accusation belongs to the enemy. Intercession belongs to covenant.

Imagine this. A paycheck is lost. Hours get cut. Bills are stacking. You sit down together and you begin like this:

"Father, in Jesus' name, we acknowledge what's in front of us. We're not pretending. We see the numbers. We see the deadlines. We see the pressure. But before we pick up calculators, we lift our hands. You are our source. You are our covering. You are our inheritance. We refuse to let this moment divide our house. We refuse to speak death over each other. We refuse to bow down to fear. Lord, give us wisdom. Show us the adjustments we need to make. Show us the pride that needs to break. Show us the lesson that's in this pressure. And let this be a testimony, not a tomb. We thank You in advance for provision because You are not discovering this today. *You saw it before we did. Be glorified in this. Amen."*

Start there. Before budgeting, start there.

That prayer does three critical things. First, it puts God above the crisis. Second, it puts you and your spouse on the same team instead of putting each other on trial. And third, it invites instruction.

Because yes, after you pray, there are practical next steps.

Walking by faith does not mean pretending the light bill doesn't exist. Trusting God does not mean being reckless or irresponsible. Sometimes trusting God looks like humility. Sometimes trusting God looks like downsizing. Sometimes trusting God looks like saying, "Cable is a luxury, not a necessity. We'll cut it for a season." Sometimes trusting God looks like saying, "We don't need both cars right now. We'll sell one." Sometimes trusting God looks like saying, "We love this apartment, but this is not the time to protect an image. This is the time to protect our covenant. We'll move. We'll regroup. We'll rebuild."

Here is where many believers stumble: pride.

We will hold on to an apartment we can no longer afford because we're worried what people will say. We will keep a car note that's strangling us because we don't want the embarrassment of saying, "They came and got it." We will refuse to move in with family temporarily because we've convinced ourselves that "a grown man doesn't do that," or "a grown woman doesn't come back home."

Listen to me with love: pride has a way of redirecting our lives when we cling to things instead of choosing humility. God is not shaming you; He is freeing you. Sometimes God says, "Let that go," not because He wants you small, but because He's preparing you for expansion, and your current identity is too wrapped up in things. He cannot promote ego. He will promote stewardship. So, in order to keep your heart, which He loves, from worshiping status and image, He will allow temporary reduction to build permanent humility.

Some of us have never experienced true need in adulthood. We've always had enough. And because of that, a quiet arrogance can form. That arrogance may not show up as obvious pride toward people. It may show up as spiritual pride: "That could never be me. I'd never be in that position. I'd never be in that situation." So God, in His mercy, may allow certain savings to run out, certain cushions to thin, and certain comforts to loosen, not to humiliate you, but to refine you. To remove the pride that would have corrupted you at the next level.

If you ignore Him in that moment, if you dig your heels in and say, "We're going to force this to work. We're going to borrow. We're going to swipe the cards. We're going to take a bad loan just to keep the image alive," you may preserve the appearance of stability for a little while, but what you're actually doing is delaying deliverance. And what could have been a short season of adjustment becomes a long season of circling the same mountain.

It is the story of Israel in the wilderness. God was ready to move them, but their mindset was not ready to move with Him. So they walked in circles. Some of us are walking in financial circles, not because God has not made a way out, but because pride has us ignoring His exit signs.

I will share something personal with you, because I will never teach you something I have not experienced in my own life.

I am from the Bahamas. I grew up in a home where, like many of you, we faced seasons when we did not have what other people had. I remember being teased about clothes. I remember what it felt like to buy my shoes from the grocery store or wear the least expensive uniforms. Children can be cruel, even when they do not mean to be.

I remember how that teasing made me burn inside. And in that burning, something awakened in me. My brothers and I started selling fruit just to help meet our needs. We became young entrepreneurs out of necessity. Out of pressure, creativity was born. Out of lack, initiative was born.

Later in life, when I became an adult, I carried a lot of responsibility for my family. I wanted to make sure my nieces and nephews had what they needed. I did not want them to feel that same sting of shame I felt. So I started buying shoes, clothes, uniforms, and school essentials for them every year. I did not ask God. I simply did it out of compassion.

But compassion without wisdom can become disobedience.

I began to stretch myself beyond what God had actually graced me to carry. I was swiping to compensate for the lack of funds. I was giving from emptiness. Then it happened: My main source of income was lost. Another job cut my hours. Suddenly, I was not just giving more than I had, I no longer had enough for myself.

I felt the fear. I felt the embarrassment. I felt the tightening in my chest. I felt that voice saying, "Look at you. Grown man. Can't even hold it together." I felt that voice asking, "What will they think? What will she think? How are you still credible now?" That voice is pride pretending to be responsibility.

In that moment, God spoke to me. Not in a loud, dramatic way. Not in a way I could show off. Just a knowing in my spirit: "Let it go. Release the apartment. Put your things in storage. I am going to take you low to teach you something."

That instruction offended my flesh because my identity at that time was attached to being stable. Stable in front of people. Stable in front of family. Stable in front of the woman I loved. Stable in front of myself. Moving out felt like failure. It felt like exposure. It felt like, "Now everyone will know I could not keep it up."

But there is a difference between keeping it up and keeping it honest. So I obeyed. I put my things in storage. And for a period of time, I slept in my car.

Now hear me carefully: I am not romanticizing struggle. I am not telling you that if you love God, you have to sleep in your car. This is not about copying my story. This is about learning how God speaks to you in your story. My wilderness will not look exactly like your wilderness. Your obedience may not look like mine. Your reduction may not look like mine. Your test may not look like mine. Please do not turn someone else's testimony into a formula. God is too personal for that.

But I will tell you what happened in that season. I encountered God in a way I had never known Him before. I heard Him. I felt Him. I received strategy. I received revelation. I began to write plays, ideas, outlines, and concepts, things that later turned into ministry and work that would bless people. In the place where it looked like I had lost everything, God was actually handing me blueprints for my future.

And when that season ended, it ended suddenly. The same way the job had been taken quickly, restoration came quickly. Not only did I move out of having no place, but God gave me multiple places. What looked like subtraction was actually positioning. What looked like humiliation was actually training. What looked like the lowest point was actually the turning point.

That is what I mean when I say: You cannot judge God's process by how it feels in the middle.

In the middle, it feels like collapse. From heaven's view, it is construction.

And I want you to notice something important in that story. I did not get that breakthrough while grumbling, arguing, lashing out, or defending my ego. I got it through surrender. I got it by saying, "Lord, if this is You, then teach me. I do not want to repeat this. I do not want to circle this lesson ten more times. Let me learn what You are teaching now."

That is the posture we need in our marriages during financial hardship.

Instead of saying, "Why is this happening to us? What did you do? What did I do? Who is to blame?" shift the question. Ask, "Father, what are You teaching us? And how do You want us to respond together?"

Together. Not "me versus you." Together.

There is spiritual protection in together. There is mental protection in together. There is financial protection in together. But together only happens when both of you agree that God is still God in the middle of the mess. Together only happens when both of you agree that the true enemy is not each other. Together only happens when both of you agree that money is a tool, not a master.

The Bible says, "The love of money is the root of all evil."

Notice carefully: not money itself. The love of it. The worship of it. The bowing to it. The chasing of it. The surrendering of integrity for it. The sacrificing of peace, marriage, health, children, and calling for it. Money, in the hands of the righteous, is a servant. Money, on the throne of a fearful heart, is a tyrant.

So when money tightens, you have a decision to make as a household. Will we worship money, or will we worship God? Will we let this crisis become our identity, or will we let this crisis become our classroom? Will we let fear run the house, or will we let wisdom and love run the house?

And let me say this, because it matters. Sometimes financial hardship is not an attack. Sometimes it is simply math. Sometimes it is mismanagement. Sometimes it is poor planning, impulsive spending, emotional buying, pride-driven decisions, or living consistently beyond what we can actually sustain. In those cases, we must be honest and humble enough to say, "We need counsel. We need budgeting help. We need to sit down with someone who can teach us stewardship." There is no shame in that. That is growth.

But other times, and many of you will recognize this, what hit your house was not the result of irresponsibility. It was a wave you could not have seen coming: a sudden layoff, an industry-wide downsizing, a health event, or an economic shutdown like what the world experienced during COVID. Global events have local consequences. And when those moments come, God will often not show you ahead of time, not because He wants you blindsided, but because if you knew everything in advance, you would never build faith.

Faith is not needed where there is no unknown. Faith is required in the dark.

That is why I keep saying: The crisis is not punishment. The crisis is an invitation.

An invitation to pray differently. An invitation to communicate differently. An invitation to reorder the home. An invitation to humble pride. An invitation to return to dependence on God instead of casual agreement with Him. An invitation to teach your children, through example, how to cling to God and not to things.

Please hear this: Your children are watching how you handle crisis more than they are watching how you act when everything is fine.

If they see you panic, scream, hide from each other, shut down, blame, curse, spiral, and turn cold when money gets tight, you are discipling them in fear. You are training them to worship stability. You are teaching them by example, "When money shakes, love shakes." But if they see you gather as a family, pray, speak peace, explain honestly but calmly, make adjustments with dignity, go on a temporary plan with confidence instead of shame, and continue to show love and tenderness in the house, they are being discipled in faith. You are teaching them, "We are held by God, not by numbers."

Even your downsizing can be prophetic if you frame it in truth: "Kids, we are going to move for a while. God is repositioning us. We are following His wisdom. This is temporary. And we are going to do it together. You are safe. You are covered. We are building. Watch what God does."

That is not pretending. That is leadership. And that is how you turn what could have been a fracture into a testimony.

So when the pressure comes, because it will, here is the order:

1. First, honor God out loud. Speak it: "Lord, this is in Your hands."
2. Second, honor each other: "We are not enemies. I love you. I'm with you."
3. Third, seek instruction: "What is God asking us to release? What is God asking us to rearrange?"
4. Fourth, obey quickly. Don't drag your feet out of pride.
5. Fifth, stay soft with each other. Do not let stress harden your tone.
6. Sixth, record the journey. Write it down. What you are walking through right now is going to feed somebody later. Somebody will need the wisdom that is being formed in

> you today. Somebody will need the calm that is being built in you right now. Somebody will need to witness your marriage surviving what most marriages crumble under. Your pain is going to become somebody else's survival manual.

And lastly, give thanks. Not fake, shallow, church-performance "thanks." Real thanks:

"Father, even in this, we thank You. We don't thank You for the pain. We thank You for Your presence in the pain. We thank You that You have not abandoned us in this. We thank You that this will not break us. We thank You that You are using this to shape us, to humble us, to align us, to promote us in character before You promote us in lifestyle. We thank You that we will not bow to fear. We thank You that our children will eat from this testimony years from now. We thank You that this loss is not the end of our story. We thank You that You are still God, and that means we are still covered."

This is what it means to trust God in setback. This is what it means to overcome financial challenges together. Together is not romantic language. Together is war language. It is covenant language. It is Kingdom language.

No challenge you face is bigger than the God who called you. No number in an account has the right to define your identity. No temporary season of reduction has the right to declare final defeat over your household. You are not owned by debt. You are not owned by fear. You are not owned by other people's opinions. You are not owned by pride. You are owned by God.

And if you are owned by God, then even this, yes, even this, is working for your good.

Lolita Brown

No matter how strong a couple's spiritual foundation may be, life will always deliver moments that test the strength of that foundation. Financial pressure has a unique way of revealing what we believe, what we fear, and, most importantly, how deeply we trust God and each other. Job loss, unexpected expenses, medical emergencies, business downturns, debt, inflation, the rising cost of living, these moments can shake even the most faith-filled pair. Yet they are never meant to break us. They are divine invitations to pause, breathe, reconnect, and rise together.

A setback is not a sign that you've failed; it's a sign that you've entered a spiritual classroom. In this room, God teaches you how to steward, how to communicate, how to stand in unity, and how to trust Him more boldly than you ever have before. Couples who learn how to walk through financial storms hand in hand discover something rare: a resilience that becomes the very soil wealth grows from.

Pressure Is Preparation

Many couples panic at the first sign of financial strain, but in Scripture, pressure is almost always a precursor to promotion. Abraham and Sarah waited years for God's provision to manifest. Joseph endured betrayal, slavery, false accusation, and imprisonment, yet every setback pushed him closer to the palace of financial authority. The widow with the oil thought she had absolutely nothing until God multiplied the little she had left.

Every biblical financial struggle was not punishment; it was positioning.

So if you find yourself in the middle of a financial storm, understand this: You are not at the end of your story. You are standing in the middle of the miracle God is building.

The Enemy Always Starts With Division

When finances get tight, the first attack rarely comes against the bank account; it comes against the bond. Blame creeps in. Miscommunication intensifies. Fear whispers. Silent resentment grows. Anxiety about the future settles in the background like a storm waiting to break.

But unity is a married couple's superpower.

When you and your spouse become one voice, one team, and one prayer, you silence the enemy's access. This is the moment to slow down, take each other's hands, and remind your home:

"If God allowed it, He will also provide for it."

Financial pressure is not the time to turn on each other; it's the time to turn toward each other.

Returning to God When Money Feels Tight

Before you run to spreadsheets, apps, advisors, or banks, run to God together. Financial storms require spiritual clarity. Pray, even if it's just ten quiet minutes a day. Ask God to reveal what's beneath the surface:

Was it overspending?

Lack of planning?

An unexpected crisis?

A moment of disobedience?

A divine redirection?

Invite the Holy Spirit to cover your home with peace and strategy. Remember who God is: Provider, Sustainer, Redeemer, Restorer, and Master Strategist. He does not waste pain, pressure, or process. Every season has purpose, including this one.

And please, refuse to entertain shame. Shame suffocates solutions. Even the wealthiest couples face financial challenges. The goal isn't perfection; it's partnership with God.

Facing the Truth Without Fear

Facing the truth without fear is one of the most courageous acts a couple can practice during a financial setback. It requires looking at the numbers honestly, not emotionally, not defensively, but simply and truthfully. Where are we really? What do we have? What do we owe? What's fallen behind? What is coming due?

Truth is never a threat; it is the doorway to transformation. When you can see your reality clearly, you gain the ability to distinguish what you can handle on your own from what truly requires an expert. Budgeting, trimming expenses, selling unused items, or calling utility companies may be within your reach, while tax issues, large debt negotiations, legal concerns, or business restructuring may require professional guidance. Asking for support is not weakness; it is maturity, stewardship, and wisdom.

And once clarity comes, it's not about doing everything at once; it's about taking the first step. One payment arrangement. One honest conversation. One phone call. One new habit. Because motion, no matter how small, creates momentum.

Spiritual Tools That Shift Atmospheres

There are seasons when the financial battle is more spiritual than practical. In those seasons, couples must fight differently:

1. Pray out loud together, surrendering worry, inviting unity, asking for clarity, and acknowledging God as your Provider.

2. Fast for direction, even if it's one meal, one day, or one moment of consecration.

3. Declare God's Word over your finances, because heaven responds when His Word is released.

4. Speak unity over your home, because a united couple is an unstoppable force.

These are not rituals. They are spiritual strategies.

Practical Steps When Money Gets Tight

Financial recovery begins with stewardship, not stress. Focus on what you can control today, not the next ten years.

- Create a 30-day emergency strategy. Cut unnecessary spending. Use cash to prevent impulse purchases. Sell unused items. Protect the essentials.
- Build a simple plan for extra income. Not forever, just for the season. A few hours a week can stabilize a home quickly.
- Contact every creditor. Silence breeds crisis, but communication often brings flexibility, extensions, lower interest, or temporary relief.
- Rebuild your budget together, not based on what your life was last year, but on what your reality is right now. This is where unity is tested, but also where unity is restored.

What Real-Life Setbacks Look Like

When a job is lost, cover your home in peace. File for unemployment if necessary. Contact every bill provider. Reduce spending. Start temporary income within seven days. Pray for direction and expect God to open a door better than the one that closed.

When debt grows, release shame. Face the numbers. Choose a payoff strategy, snowball or avalanche. Consolidate if appropriate. Ask God for strategy and discipline.

When unexpected expenses hit, pause spending. Redirect funds. Create a simple 90-day recovery plan. Ask God for wisdom and creativity. He never fails to provide solutions. Setbacks are temporary. Strategy is permanent.

A Moment of Prayer Together

"Lord, we thank You that this setback is not the end of our story. Give us unity, wisdom, and supernatural strategy. Strengthen our faith and show us how to honor You with every step we take. We trust You to restore what we cannot fix on our own. In Jesus' name, Amen."

Journaling for Clarity and Connection

1. What financial challenge are we truly facing right now?
2. What emotions rise when we think about it?
3. What is God trying to teach us in this season?
4. What practical steps can we take over the next seven days?
5. Where do we need expert guidance?
6. Which Scriptures bring us peace?

Once you finish, schedule a money meeting, just twenty minutes. Choose one financial priority for the week. Reach out to one expert if needed. And begin a 30-day prayer challenge for unity and clarity.

A financial setback is not evidence that your marriage is collapsing. It is a sign that your marriage is being strengthened.

God has never brought His people into struggle without also preparing a strategy for victory. You will not remain in this season forever. You will rise, you will regroup, you will rebuild, and you will look back and say:

"This is where God shifted everything."

CHAPTER SEVEN

BUILDING WEALTH THROUGH SERVICE - HOW GIVING UNLOCKS BLESSINGS

Van Brown

There's a quiet truth I learned early in my walk with God, one that didn't come to me through a sermon, a conference, or a mentor, but through the slow unraveling of my own life: Wealth, true wealth, does not emerge from the hours we grind or the salaries we negotiate. It rises from service. It emerges from giving. It flows from stepping into the very thing God whispered over your life before you ever took your first breath.

This truth is impossible to grasp without first confronting the tension between two worlds: the world's system and God's Kingdom. For most of us, the world trained us long before we ever met the Kingdom. From childhood, the system started shaping us, nudging us toward career paths, applauding the idea of "stability," and conditioning us to chase the safest route with the highest paycheck. Our teachers asked, "What do you want to be when you grow up?" and we answered with whatever our little hearts could imagine: veterinarians, firefighters, crossing guards, astronauts. Children choose based on love and curiosity. Adults choose based on bills.

But as we grow, the innocence of our dreams gets swallowed by expectation. The system tells us to study hard, pick a major, graduate, and get a job, even if the job has nothing to do with the dream we once carried. The irony, of course, is that most people spend four years studying one thing only to spend the next forty doing something entirely different. The world's system never promised purpose. It only promised a paycheck.

Yet God never designed us for that kind of life. When He formed humanity, He didn't say, "Let them get a good salary." He said, "Let them have dominion." Dominion is not employment; it is assignment. It is ruling in the area of your calling. Even money, printed from the trees we were given authority over, was never meant to dominate us. It was meant to serve us as we serve God's purpose.

I didn't understand this until my own life fell apart. My education didn't teach it. My environment didn't model it. My family didn't discuss purpose or calling. But heartbreak, heartbreak became my teacher. After a series of painful relationships that left my heart scattered across the floor, I found myself in a quiet library searching for answers. Not answers from God, I wasn't walking with Him yet so I thought, but answers from books, psychologists, and thinkers who could help me make sense of the chaos inside me.

I read one book on love, then another, then another. Before I knew it, I was drowning in literature, hundreds of books on emotional health, communication, attachment, relationships, and identity. Page after page, revelation after revelation, I began to realize something: I wasn't just learning how to love better, I was being reshaped. Rebuilt. Restored.

And while God was rebuilding me, something unexpected began happening around me. Friends started seeking me out. Couples invited me into their living rooms. People, broken, confused, frustrated, began asking for counsel, not because I advertised myself, not because I was certified, and not because I knew all the answers. They came because healing was first identified in me, and they could feel it. I wasn't trying to build a brand or launch a business. I was simply serving from the place God had rebuilt in me. And each time I sat across from a couple on the verge of collapse and watched God stitch them back together, each time I witnessed clarity return to a clouded mind or forgiveness soften a hardened heart, something in me awakened. It was purpose. It was calling. And it came wrapped inside the pain I once thought would destroy me.

Years passed, and what began as quiet service turned into a ministry, one I never saw coming. My wife and I now travel the world mentoring couples, counseling leaders, guiding families, and stewarding resources in ways that still humble me. Yes, we run businesses. Yes, we have clients who pay for our time. But God funds our lives through obeying His whispers.

Even now, with all that we have accomplished, the majority of what we do is still rooted in giving. We take on couples who cannot afford our services because impact means more to us than invoices. We intentionally dedicate a portion of our schedule to pro bono mentorship, investing in the next generation of young men and women because we believe guidance and wisdom should be shared, not reserved only for those who can afford it. We serve our church, not for applause, not for payment, but because service is the heartbeat of the Kingdom.

And in all of this, God has never failed us. Opportunities find us. Partnerships locate us. Favor surrounds us before we even ask, not because we chase wealth, but because we chase purpose. Wealth follows service like a shadow that cannot detach itself from the one who leads.

This is the paradox of God's Kingdom:

The more you give, the more you gain.

The more you serve, the higher you rise.

The more you release, the more God trusts you with.

The world calls it irrational. Heaven calls it law.

The world calls it loss. Heaven calls it seed.

Everything we have belongs to God. We are merely stewards.

When He nudges us to bless someone, a young student sleeping in his car, a family struggling to keep their home, a widow counting coins to buy groceries, that nudge is never just about them. It is about us. About whether God can trust us not to grip His blessings so tightly that our knuckles turn white and our hearts grow small.

Some people struggle to give because, deep down, they believe everything they have came from their own strength. They call themselves "self-made." They forget who fed them as children, who prayed for them, who taught them, who opened doors for them, and who encouraged them when they were empty. They forget that even survival required the hands of others.

A man who believes he built himself has no understanding of the God who carried him.

But the man who knows that God is the source, that man gives freely. That man serves joyfully. That man builds wealth effortlessly because his wealth is rooted in purpose, not pride.

Every day, my wife and I watch the ripple effects of service. Couples message us years later saying, "You saved our marriage." Young people write us saying, "Your words kept me from giving up." Families tell us that they pray together now, communicate better now, and dream again now, all because of a seed we sowed years before.

And every time I hear those words, I am reminded of this: The healing, the restoration, and the families made whole are the real wealth. Not the bank accounts, the properties, or the investments, but the impact we leave behind. Wealth is found in legacy, service, obedience to God's voice, and fulfilling the purpose He placed inside us.

And money? Money becomes the silent witness of a life lived well.

So when I speak about building wealth through service, I'm not giving theory. I'm giving testimony. I'm telling you that your greatest breakthrough won't come from chasing money; it will come from saying yes to the thing God placed inside you long before this world trained you to forget it.

Your calling is not random.

Your gift is not accidental.

Your pain was not wasted.

And your purpose, your true purpose, is the place where your wealth has been hiding.

If you strip away the noise, sit still long enough to hear God's voice, and dare to serve in the area of your calling, you will unlock a life that not only blesses you but blesses generations after you. Because wealth, in the Kingdom, has never been about what you accumulate. It has always been about who you become and who you lift while becoming. And when you live that way, you won't have to worry about money. Money will always know where to find you.

Lolita Brown

Most couples desire wealth. What many do not realize is that wealth does not respond first to effort; it responds to alignment. There are spiritual laws that govern increase, just as surely as there are financial ones. And among them, one principle stands firm, consistent, and undeniable: Giving unlocks blessing. Not occasionally. Not only when it feels comfortable. Not only after overflow appears. Giving works every time it is done with intention, unity, and a sincere heart.

In God's economy, your future is not built by your salary alone. It is shaped by your seed. Generosity becomes the doorway through which divine opportunity, provision, and favor flow. And when a husband and wife learn to give together, something powerful happens within the marriage itself: Unity deepens. Vision expands. Trust grows. Their relationship becomes something God can confidently increase.

Open Hands, Open Futures

The world teaches us to protect, to grip tightly, and to secure ourselves by holding on. God teaches the opposite. In His Kingdom, wealth grows when hands open, not when they clench. Couples who build lasting wealth understand that giving is not loss; it is placement. Every seed released is an investment into something larger than the present moment. Whether you are tithing, supporting a ministry, blessing a family, or sowing into a cause close to your heart, you are participating in a divine exchange. A seed may leave your hand, but it never leaves your life. It moves forward and waits for you. Just as a farmer places seed into soil, trusting that something unseen is taking place, couples who give trust that spiritual laws are at work beyond what the eye can immediately observe. Giving requires faith because growth begins underground.

The Quiet Work of the Seed

Picture a farmer standing in an empty field, holding seed. He can preserve what he has and remain exactly where he is, or he can release it and trust the process of increase. Once the seed is planted, the field looks unchanged. There is no instant evidence. No visible reward. Yet beneath the soil, the seed is doing its work, breaking open, taking root, drawing nourishment, and preparing for multiplication. This is how giving works within a marriage.

Often, couples sow and continue living their lives without immediate proof that anything has shifted. But something has. A harvest begins the moment the seed is released. Timing varies, but the outcome does not, provided the heart remains right, the sowing remains consistent, and faith is not undermined by doubt or complaint. Wise farmers do not sow once and stop. They sow season after season. And couples who build wealth the same way, steadily and faithfully, experience increase that is both sustainable and meaningful.

Sowing Is a Law, Not a Suggestion

Scripture reminds us that whatever is sown will be reaped. This is not simply a verse; it is a principle woven into creation itself. We see it everywhere. When you sow time, you reap opportunity. When you sow love, you reap connection. When you sow service, doors open. And when you sow financially, provision responds. What makes God's system extraordinary is not addition, but multiplication.

Seed is never returned in equal measure. It comes back expanded, often in ways you did not anticipate. A small act of obedience can unlock a season of unexpected increase. A single moment of generosity can shift the trajectory of a family's future. But reaping is impossible without sowing. Wealth, spiritual, relational, or financial, cannot grow where nothing has been planted.

Giving Together Changes the Marriage

There is a unique power released when couples give in agreement. When a husband and wife decide together where and how to sow, their hearts align. Conversations deepen. Vision sharpens. Trust strengthens. Giving becomes a shared language of faith. It teaches discipline. It teaches sacrifice. It teaches how to hear God together. And it dismantles the very things that restrict abundance: fear, selfishness, and scarcity.

Many prosperous couples, across cultures and backgrounds, attribute their success not merely to strategy, but to service. They understand that generosity keeps the heart clear and the hands open. And God entrusts more to those who steward resources without clinging to them.

Deposits That Outlive You

Scripture speaks of storing treasure in heaven, not as metaphor, but as reality. Every act of giving is a deposit into an account that operates beyond earthly systems. Wise couples do not give randomly. They give intentionally. Just as financial accounts require structure and planning, generosity does as well. When giving is purposeful, it becomes a form of spiritual wealth management.

Where you sow matters.

Why you sow matters.

Consistency matters.

Each seed carries an assignment. Sometimes that assignment is obedience alone. Other times, it is tied to a breakthrough, a future goal, or a dream yet unrealized. But no seed is wasted when it is sown in faith.

A Marriage That Gives Grows

Giving does not impoverish a marriage; it enriches it. The world warns against scarcity. God invites abundance. Couples who embrace generosity discover that their giving becomes their stability. Their seed becomes their future. Their obedience becomes generational blessing. You are not simply married to each other. You are married to purpose. Married to calling. Married to Kingdom principles that, when honored, produce increase far beyond what effort alone could accomplish. And generosity is one of the keys that unlocks it all.

A Prayer for Generous Hearts

Father, we come before You as one, united in love, united in purpose, and grateful for every resource You have entrusted to us. Teach us to give with wisdom, joy, and faith. Remove fear and scarcity from our hearts, and help us recognize the ground You are calling us to sow into. We declare that every seed we release is moving into our future, producing favor, provision, and opportunity for our family. Strengthen our unity as we give together. Let our generosity draw us closer and position us for greater responsibility. We thank You for the harvest already in motion. May our marriage be a testimony that when we give, You multiply.

In Jesus' name, Amen.

Reflection Questions

1. How do we personally view giving, as a loss or as an investment in our future?

___

___

___

___

2. In what ways has generosity strengthened or challenged our marriage so far?

___

___

___

___

3. Are we giving intentionally and consistently, or only when it feels comfortable?

___

___

___

___

___

4. How aligned are we as a couple in where and why we sow?

____

____

____

5. What fears, if any, affect how freely we give?

____

____

____

6. Where have we seen past seeds produce unexpected blessing or opportunity?

____

____

____

____

7. What is one step we can take together to grow in generosity this season?

____

____

____

____

CHAPTER EIGHT

GENERATIONAL WEALTH - LEAVING A LEGACY OF FAITH AND PURPOSE

Van Brown

There's a moment in every man's life when he begins to realize that everything he is building, everything he is fighting for, and everything he is becoming is no longer just about him. Something shifts quietly, steadily, almost imperceptibly, until one day he wakes up and understands: I am someone's history. I am the story my children will tell. I am the memory my grandchildren will interpret. I am the foundation someone who has never met me will one day stand on.

I didn't always think this way. I grew into it, the way a man grows into his name or the way a tree grows into its roots: slowly, and only after surviving seasons that tried to uproot him. But it was during a period of intense prayer, mentorship, and internal wrestling that God made something abundantly clear to me: Just as I call Him Father, there will be generations after me who call me theirs. And if that is true, then nothing I do can be governed by how I feel. It must be governed by what God said.

And God said something profound, so profound that it reverberates through the spiritual constitution of every believer willing to listen: "*A good man leaves an inheritance to his children's children.*"

He didn't say a wealthy man.

He didn't say a perfect man.

He didn't say an influential man.

He said a *good* man.

Goodness, in Heaven's eyes, is not merely morality; it is stewardship, foresight, discipline, self-governance, and spiritual maturity. When the Father speaks of a good man, He is referring to a man who understands that everything in his hands is a seed, and every seed is meant to outlive him.

When I first meditated on that Scripture, I didn't hear it as a command. I heard it as a revelation of God's heart toward humanity. God knew the men He created. He knew we would have the tendency to protect only what we could see, to hold everything close, to guard what was ours, and to ignore the generations not yet born. Without God, men are not naturally generational; we are naturally in the now. We think in days, not decades. We think in moments, not movements. We think in pleasure, not purpose.

And so the Father placed this principle in Scripture as a safeguard. A man without God focuses on temporal things, while a man with God sees beyond his life and looks forward. A man with God is required to look forward. And when you see the world through that lens, everything changes.

Most people hear the words "generational wealth" and immediately think of finances: bank accounts, properties, trust funds, stocks, and a stable, predictable future. And yes, those things matter. I believe in them, and I invest in them. But they are not the foundation of generational wealth; they are the fruit.

When Jesus walked the earth, the most valuable thing He left behind wasn't money, property, or any of the things men fight over today. He left a culture: a way of thinking, a way of living, a way of loving, a way of forgiving, a way of believing, and a way of praying. He left a Kingdom, a philosophy of life anchored not in possessions, but in posture.

Generational wealth is not first about what you leave in their hands.

It is about what you leave in their minds.

It is not primarily about assets; it is about attitude.

It is not just inheritance; it is impartation.

The truth is, everything you do is forming the mindset of the generations coming after you. The food you eat, the habits you cultivate, the friendships you keep, the prayers you pray, the books you read, the way you discipline yourself, these things are seeds. And whether we realize it or not, our children and grandchildren will harvest the consequences or the blessings of those seeds.

I learned this revelation right before my wife and I married. I had been deep in mentorship, prayer, fasting, and wrestling with the weight of what it meant to be a husband and a father. I asked God how I could ensure I didn't simply pass down my last name, but also my wisdom, my character, my faith, and my clarity.

And the Lord said something that has followed me every day since:

"Live in a way that you would be honored to hand your choices to the next generation; let every action be worthy of inheritance, and only do what you would be willing to see repeated in those who come after you."

That shook me.

It meant the question of righteousness was no longer just, "Is this right or wrong?" but, "Can I pass this to my children's children without shame?" That one question shifted everything: my entertainment choices, my friendships, my discipline, my relationships, my spending habits, my prayer life, my integrity, my emotional responses, and my spiritual posture. Because if I couldn't pass something on, then it had no place in the foundation of my family. Generational wealth requires this level of thinking.

When you begin to see yourself through the lens of legacy, pleasure stops being the compass of your decisions. Purpose begins guiding you. You stop consuming things that do not honor your body. You pull away from addictions that collapse your future. You let go of relationships that diminish your spiritual strength. You refuse to engage in behaviors that shorten your days or pollute your mind. You even change the way you speak because every word you utter can live forever in the digital archives of this world.

We forget that long after we abandon an argument, long after we outgrow a season, and long after we mature beyond the immaturity of our twenties or thirties, something we said in passing may still live online. And while we have moved on, our children may one day pay the price for the impression we left behind in anger, immaturity, or ignorance.

Generational wealth requires restraint.

It requires accountability.

It requires that you live today as though someone you love will inherit your decisions tomorrow.

Because they will.

The decisions you make behind closed doors are writing the story your grandchildren will read. I once heard a man say he could not be bothered with the future because "those kids will have to figure it out on their own." And I said to myself, that is not a father speaking; that is a man still trapped in the wounds of his own youth. Most fathers are simply duplications of their fathers. Our behaviors are often relics of the patterns we witnessed.

When I wrote my first book, I had to confront this painful truth. My father raised me with silence, never complimenting me, never telling me he was proud. He was not a bad man. He was mirroring what he received. It was not until after he passed that his best friend told me how much my father bragged about me when I was not there. And even now, when I return home to the Bahamas, his friends treat me with a tenderness, generosity, and respect that were built on the wealth my father left behind, not financial wealth, but the wealth of friendship, loyalty, and character.

That is generational wealth, too.

You don't only pass down money.

You pass down reputation.

You pass down relationships.

You pass down the fragrance of your character.

And your children walk into rooms already lifted or lowered by the memory of your name. This is why a man who seeks generational wealth must govern not only his money, but also his mind, his mouth, and his character.

When I decided to propose to my wife, I was led to write a fifty-year plan. Not because we were obsessed with control, but because we understood something: Our children's children deserved clarity. They deserved to know how we thought about family, how we viewed covenant, how we resolved conflict, how we made decisions, how we sought God, how we built our businesses, how we forgave each other, and how we protected our love.

Every family needs a manual. Not a list of rules, but a blueprint of philosophy.

How do we treat one another?

How do we speak to one another?

How do we handle disagreements?

How do we value God?

How do we parent?

How do we sacrifice?

How do we stand in faith during crisis?

How do we choose purpose over pleasure?

When you document these things, not as a perfect person but as an honest one, you give your children something money could never buy: a mind that can survive any economic collapse. You give them a strategy for life. A clarity of thought. A posture of faith. A rhythm of wisdom. You give them the mind of Christ in a language they understand: your own testimony.

I often wonder how many of today's problems could have been avoided if the generation before us had written down their wisdom instead of burying it with them. How many marriages could have been spared? How many financial pitfalls avoided? How many young men could have walked straighter? How many young women could have walked wiser? We think generational wealth is stored in bank accounts. But real generational wealth is stored in journals, prayers, decisions, wisdom, and discipline.

Money can disappear in a crisis. Mindset cannot. Faith cannot. Courage cannot. Wisdom cannot. A trust fund cannot rebuild a man's soul. But a father's written testimony can.

I imagine my grandchildren one day reading pages of my journals and seeing the raw truth of my journey: the days I wanted to quit but stayed because legacy demanded it; the seasons where God was silent and I learned that silence is not absence; the nights I forgave people who didn't deserve forgiveness because bitterness was too expensive a burden to hand to my children; the decisions I made to protect my future children from addictions I saw destroy others; the prayers I whispered for their marriages before they were ever conceived; and the moments I chose discipline over pleasure, not because I was strong, but because I had them in mind.

This is wealth.

This is inheritance.

This is legacy.

When a man leaves behind not just money, but his mind, his faith, his character, his ethics, and his spiritual walk, he leaves behind a blueprint that cannot be taken from his lineage.

Men were never designed to pass down only financial

provision, yet many never pause long enough to pass down wisdom. They leave assets behind without the understanding required to sustain them. They hand over businesses, but not the character needed to run them. They leave real estate, but not the resilience to endure seasons of loss. They provide resources, but never impart revelation. And when wisdom is absent, wealth becomes fragile. Buildings crumble. Businesses fall apart. Inheritances evaporate. And the very blessing meant to secure a future becomes a burden that curses a generation. All because a man placed more emphasis on what he could put in his children's hands than what he should have placed in their hearts.

Scripture teaches us that wisdom is the principal thing, and without it, even the greatest inheritance becomes dangerous. Generational wealth, therefore, is far more than financial strategy; it is a way of life. It is the clarity to see beyond the moment, the intentionality to build for a future you may never witness, and the discipline to deny yourself pleasures today that could destroy someone you love tomorrow. It is the quiet courage to say, "This ends with me," so your children don't have to wrestle the demons you fought. It is the humility to acknowledge, "I wasn't given a blueprint, but I will write a full one for the generations coming after me." It is the deep, unwavering desire for your grandchildren to know God not just through the Scriptures they read, but through the stories of how He carried you.

Real generational wealth is the documentation of faith, the preservation of purpose, the recording of wisdom, the modeling of character, the demonstration of love, and the kind of integrity that is practiced in private long before it is ever recognized in public.

I often imagine the day my grandchildren will stand on a stage, sit at a boardroom table, kneel beside their bed in prayer, or battle through a quiet season of despair. And I pray that in those moments, something within them rises, something ancient, something holy, something woven into their very being by the generations who came before them. Not my money, my status, or even the reputation attached to my name, but the deeper inheritance: my mind, my faith, my discipline, my revelation, my devotion, my obedience, and my relationship with God.

That is the kind of wealth no crisis can dissolve, no economy can steal, no enemy can undermine, and no circumstance can shake. That is the inheritance of a good man.

So yes, build the businesses, establish the trusts, buy the properties, and grow the assets. But never forget that the greatest work is the mindset you leave behind, the faith you lived out, the principles you embodied, the stories you shared, the manual you wrote through your choices, and the blueprint that shaped you. These are the treasures that allow generations you will never meet to walk confidently in the footsteps you left behind.

For in the end, the greatest wealth a man gives is not what he places into his children's hands, but what he cultivates within their hearts and mine.

And may God grant us the wisdom, the courage, and the discipline to build that kind of generational wealth, wealth that echoes in Heaven and reverberates through the earth long after our names have slipped quietly into memory.

Lolita Brown

When God blesses a marriage, His intention is never limited to the two people standing at the altar. A Kingdom marriage is designed to carry weight far beyond the present moment. It is meant to reach forward into children, grandchildren, and generations yet unborn. True wealth was never meant to stop with us.

In my years of managing wealth, I've learned this simple truth: What you build quietly today becomes the inheritance someone else lives in tomorrow. Every decision you make as a couple, how you earn, how you save, how you give, and how you plan, creates a pattern. That pattern becomes a legacy. In God's eyes, wealth is not measured only by what you accumulate. It is measured by what you prepare to pass on. Most couples are focused on surviving the present, paying bills, managing responsibilities, and getting through the next season. Few stop to ask the deeper questions. Few take the time to look fifty years ahead and consider how today's choices will shape tomorrow's outcomes. Yet every blessing carries an assignment. And that assignment is larger than comfort. It is about building something that outlives you.

Wealth With Purpose

Generational wealth is often misunderstood as money alone. But money, by itself, is never enough. I have seen families inherit millions and lose it all within a generation, not because they lacked resources, but because they lacked wisdom. True generational wealth is layered. It includes values. It includes vision. It includes discipline, faith, and understanding. Money becomes powerful only when it is anchored to purpose.

A couple committed to generational wealth thinks differently. They pay attention not just to what they own, but to what they are modeling. They understand that children inherit more than assets; they inherit habits, attitudes, and beliefs. The way you handle money teaches long before your words ever do. Your wealth is not just the accounts in your name. It is the mindset you pass down. It is the principles your children grow up watching. It is the faith that frames every financial decision in your home. When wealth is aligned with purpose, it becomes a tool, not a trap. It creates options, stability, and influence that extend far beyond your lifetime.

Thinking Beyond Today

One of the most powerful shifts a couple can make is learning to think long-term, not just next year, not just retirement, but generations. I've sat with families who intentionally mapped out their future decades in advance. They talked about their children and grandchildren with clarity. They discussed property they wanted to own, businesses they wanted to build, and values they wanted their family name to represent. They planned not only for growth, but for protection, understanding that stewardship includes preserving what you build.

This kind of vision requires unity. It requires patience. It requires faith. Most of all, it requires the belief that your marriage was called to steward more than a lifestyle. It was called to steward a legacy.

Protecting What You Build

One of the clearest ways a couple declares generational intent is through structure. Establishing a family trust is not simply a legal step. It is a statement of vision. A trust allows you to protect assets, guide how wealth is used, and ensure that what you've built remains aligned with your values long after you are gone. It brings order. It brings clarity. It removes confusion and unnecessary strain from future generations. When couples take this step, they are saying something powerful to their children: Your future matters. We are thinking ahead for you. That kind of preparation is an act of love.

The Real Inheritance

Money can be spent. Wealth without wisdom can disappear. But values endure. The greatest inheritance you can leave your children is not simply financial; it is instructional. Teaching them how to honor God with resources, how to save and grow responsibly, how to give generously, and how to think long-term prepares them to steward whatever comes into their hands. When children understand both the principles of wealth and the posture of stewardship, they are equipped not just to receive, but to multiply. Money responds to mindset. And mindset is taught.

Faith and Finances at Home

Teaching children about money does not require perfection. It requires presence. Talk openly. Let them see money as something to manage, not fear. Invite them into age-appropriate conversations. Allow them to observe budgeting, giving, saving, and planning. Let them watch you pray over decisions and seek God's guidance.

Children learn by example first. What they see modeled consistently becomes normal. And when they are allowed to earn, manage, and make small decisions, they build confidence and discipline that will serve them for life. Legacy becomes real when it is discussed, not hidden.

Building Intentionally

Legacy does not happen by accident. It is built decision by decision, season by season. Families who thrive long-term create space for vision. They talk. They plan. They revisit their goals. They establish rhythms that keep faith and purpose at the center of their financial lives.

They choose projects that matter, whether that's property, a family business, a scholarship, or something uniquely aligned with their calling.

What matters most is intention.

Reflection Questions

1. When we think about wealth, what do we want it to represent for our family beyond money?

___

___

___

___

2. Are our current financial habits aligned with the legacy we want to leave?

___

___

___

___

3. How intentionally do we invite God into our financial decisions as a couple?

___

___

___

___

___

4. What values do we want our children to inherit through our example?

____

____

____

5. Are we planning mainly for today, or are we preparing for future generations?

____

____

____

6. What systems or safeguards have we put in place to protect what we are building?

____

____

____

____

7. What is one intentional step we can take together this year to strengthen our family's legacy?

____

____

____

CHAPTER NINE

STAYING SPIRITUALLY GROUNDED WHILE PURSUING FINANCIAL SUCCESS

Van Brown

One of the most sobering revelations I have learned in this life is that crisis, more than prosperity, comfort, or routine, has a way of exposing what we truly believe. Even people who claim no belief at all will instinctively cry out to God when life hangs in the balance. I have seen atheists whisper prayers in hospital rooms. I have seen skeptics cry out for mercy when they thought their last breath was approaching. And I have watched, in the aftermath of natural disasters, as news anchors who never mention God in their regular broadcasting suddenly end their segments with, "Our thoughts and prayers are with the families." It is fascinating that in a nation that prides itself on pushing God out of its schools, government, public squares, and daily language, when tragedy strikes, the collective human response still reaches upward.

What this teaches us is simple: The spiritual life cannot be treated like a coat we put on in the winter and store away in the spring. Whether a person is climbing the mountain of financial success or sleeping beneath a bridge with no food to eat, their spiritual grounding remains the most critical aspect of their existence. The pursuit of God was never meant to be seasonal, situational, or circumstantial. Heaven is not populated with people who needed something; it is filled with people who loved Someone. That truth reshapes everything. It means that my spiritual life must remain my anchor whether my business is flourishing or failing, whether my accounts are overflowing or empty, whether I am celebrated or forgotten. Success must never become the substitute for presence. Prosperity must never become the replacement for intimacy. And influence must never become the idol that replaces our Father.

At some point in your journey, you must decide who you are going to be. Life will certainly hand you opportunities, setbacks, open doors, and closed ones. But the decision of how you will live, how you will walk, how you will think, and who you will become, comes from seeking God's mind about who you are. If indeed we believe that we are sons and daughters of God, then we must also believe that He has placed within us the authority to determine the posture of our lives. He handed us this truth plainly: "I have come that you may have life, and life more abundantly." If abundance is available, then the question becomes whether we will align with the rhythm required to sustain it.

Staying Spiritually Grounded While Pursuing Financial Success

Overworking ourselves into exhaustion is not abundance. Accumulating wealth at the cost of losing our marriages and damaging our children is not abundance. Acquiring status while abandoning spiritual stability is not abundance. Real abundance is hearing the voice of your Father and following it with discipline, humility, and intimacy. Real abundance is walking through seasons of success and downturn without the shifting sands of emotion altering your devotion. Real abundance is establishing a rhythm with God that cannot be disrupted by the pressures of life.

To love God with all your heart, soul, and mind is not a suggestion; it is the posture that sets the atmosphere for everything else to prosper. That posture requires intimacy. Intimacy requires sacrifice, sacrifice of sleep, sacrifice of ego, sacrifice of distraction, and sacrifice of your need to control. It requires meditation, not the emptying of the mind that the world teaches, but the filling of the mind with the presence of God. It requires prayer and fasting. It requires mentorship and accountability. It requires the humility to sit under someone who has traveled further than you have and learn the ways of God, not just the works of God.

I learned something years ago from Dr. Myles that changed the trajectory of my spiritual maturity: “God knows more than He told you.” That one sentence carries an entire universe of truth. God will give you glimpses of your future, flashes of your calling, whispers of your destiny, but He will never hand you the full picture. Why? Because the process of seeking Him is how we grow. If the full picture were revealed at once, we would have no incentive to pursue His voice daily. The wise person learns to seek God continually because they understand that every new season requires an updated version of themselves, a version that only comes from intimacy with God. I believe this is where Solomon faltered. Wisdom without continued intimacy becomes arrogance. And arrogance, once it takes root, distances the heart from God.

There is nothing sinful or unrighteous about wanting your business to prosper, your investments to grow, or your resources to multiply. These things are perfectly aligned with the life God desires for us. What becomes dangerous is when those desires begin to eclipse our devotion. When you start to measure your worth by your possessions, when your conversations revolve only around who can elevate your status, when the people you reach out to are based solely on what they can offer you, and when your prayer life shrinks because you believe you can handle things on your own, you have unknowingly placed mammon where God belongs.

The shift is subtle. It is rarely loud or obvious. It begins with a decline in prayer here, a neglected devotion there, a distancing from community, lukewarm worship, and a heart that was once tender becoming increasingly numb. Before long, you are working harder than ever, but feeling emptier than ever. You are earning more, but loving less. You are expanding your influence, but shrinking in your intimacy with God. Vanity is a silent thief; it takes without making a sound.

Look across the landscapes of entertainment, sports, business, and culture, and you can see this pattern everywhere. People who once praised God passionately now speak His name only as a branding tool, or not at all. People who once invited the presence of God into every decision now operate purely from intellect, strategy, and ambition. People who once were deeply rooted in spiritual community now orbit in circles where God is an afterthought, a footnote, or a marketing accessory. They did not abandon God in one day; it was a slow drift, a subtle erosion of affection, and a gradual shifting of priorities.

This is why spiritual rhythm matters. You need mentors who can look you in the eye and ask, "How is your heart? How is your devotion? Are you still praying? Are you still listening to God? Or has something else taken His place?" You need people who are not impressed by your success and not intimidated by your calling, people who care more about your soul than your status.

Because God is a gentleman. He will not force you to stay close. If you drift, He will allow the distance. If you pursue Him, He will reveal Himself. The entire relationship hinges on desire. He did not command salvation because He refuses forced love. Instead He commanded love, love for Him and love for your neighbor, because that is the fabric that creates Kingdom citizens.

This is why you must continually examine yourself. Look at your relationships. Look at your habits. Look at your consumption. Look at the things you pursue when no one is watching. Look at the thoughts that dominate your mind. Because whatever you chase becomes your god. And if you are not pursuing God while chasing success, success will eventually consume you.

We must build a rhythm where God is not an emergency contact, but our daily dwelling place. In the car, we turn our hearts toward Him. In meetings, we ask for His grace. In silence, we honor Him. In moments of breakthrough, we bless Him. In seasons of famine, we trust Him. Gratitude becomes the language of our soul, not because we have everything we want, but because we know that even where we are is a miracle compared to where we could have been.

We serve a God who desires closeness. He desires admiration. He desires devotion. He desires a partnership with you that is not based on what you need, but rooted in who He is. When you approach Him from that posture, crisis cannot dismantle you. Success cannot distract you. The noise of the world cannot drown out His voice. You remain steady, grounded, and anchored. That is spiritual rhythm. And without it, you may gain the world but lose yourself.

As your financial ladder climbs, as opportunities expand, and as influence grows, whisper continually:

"Father, help me. Keep me near. Let me not forget You. Let me not become intoxicated by the praise of men. Let me not be seduced by the illusion of self-sufficiency. Anchor me in Your presence. Let Your ways be my compass. Let Your voice be my guide."

This is the posture that guards your soul from the intoxication of success.

This is the posture that ensures mammon never becomes your master.

This is the posture that keeps you from spiritual bankruptcy.

This is the posture that guarantees longevity, stability, and divine instruction.

For the God who gave you the vision wants to walk with you through its fulfillment. But you must desire Him more than the fulfillment itself.

And when you live this way, when you cultivate intimacy, pursue His heart, and commit to remaining anchored no matter how high you climb, you will discover what success truly feels like. Not the applause of men. Not the size of your bank account. Not the accolades of your industry. But the quiet assurance that you have not lost yourself in the process of becoming who He called you to be.

That is success.

That is rhythm.

That is wealth.

And that is the life God designed for you from the very beginning.

Lolita Brown

Building wealth is honorable. Wanting increase is not a flaw; it is often a reflection of responsibility, vision, and the desire to provide. Scripture makes it clear that God takes pleasure in the prosperity of His people. But prosperity becomes dangerous when it begins to replace the very foundation it was meant to support. The true test of a Kingdom couple is not whether they can build wealth. It is whether they can sustain it without losing themselves.

You can succeed without becoming prideful.

You can grow without drifting.

You can prosper and remain surrendered.

Real prosperity is never measured only by what you accumulate. It is revealed in what remains steady as increase comes: the health of your faith, the strength of your marriage, and the clarity of your purpose. Wealth built the Kingdom way is ordered. It is balanced. And it is rooted.

When Wealth Is in Its Proper Place

Money is meant to serve, not to lead. Many couples begin their financial journey with pure intentions, but along the way, the climb can become consuming. Goals grow. Pressure increases. The noise gets louder. Slowly, success can begin to speak more clearly than God's voice if you are not careful.

Kingdom wealth requires balance. It requires awareness. And

it requires a commitment to keep God first consistently, not occasionally.

Wealth is a blessing when you steward it. It becomes a burden when it begins to steward you. Couples who remain grounded are willing to pause and reflect. They ask themselves honest questions, not out of fear, but out of wisdom. They check in with their hearts just as often as they check their accounts. They understand that financial growth should never outpace spiritual growth.

Ambition That Remains Submitted

Vision is not the enemy. Desire is not the enemy. Ambition, when submitted, is a gift. The danger is not in wanting more; it is in forgetting why you wanted more in the first place. Couples who build well understand that success must remain anchored in humility. They recognize that they are stewards, not owners. They allow discipline to shape their decisions rather than letting money dictate their values. And they pay attention to their spiritual health, especially when momentum increases quickly.

Abundance can distract just as easily as lack. Comparison, exhaustion, pride, and busyness often appear when things are going well. This is why staying spiritually grounded is not optional. It is protection. It is the anchor that keeps a marriage steady when success accelerates.

Protecting What Matters Most

It is possible to reach every financial milestone and still feel distant from one another. It is possible to build a legacy and still have a home filled with tension. Wealth cannot compensate for disconnection. Money is replaceable. Unity is not.

This is why marriage must remain central. Before business plans, investment strategies, and long-term goals, there must be intentional care for the relationship itself. Couples who thrive understand that wealth is meant to support the marriage, not compete with it.

They protect time.

They protect communication.

They protect spiritual alignment.

They remember to enjoy one another outside of planning, numbers, and responsibility. Because wealth built at the expense of the home is not wealth, it is loss.

Following God, Not Just Strategy

The wisest couples do not attempt to lead their financial journey alone. They follow God in it. They seek Him for direction, timing, and clarity. They invite Him into decisions. They pray and fast together. They quiet the noise when discernment is needed.

When God is welcomed into your finances, He begins to order things you cannot see. He removes what is misaligned. He reveals what has been hidden. He opens doors that no amount of strategy could force and closes doors that would have cost you more than you realized. *Divine wisdom is the greatest asset a couple can possess. Everything else builds upon it.*

A Rhythm That Keeps You Aligned

Grounded couples create rhythm. Not rigid rules, but intentional moments of alignment. They check in with one another regularly, not just about money, but about faith, connection, and purpose. They talk about what God is saying, how they are feeling, and where adjustments may be needed.

This rhythm keeps ego in check, priorities clear, and hearts aligned. It is far easier to course-correct weekly than to repair years of drift.

A Life Where Faith and Wealth Agree

You already have what you need to build wealth the Kingdom way. You have foundation. You have faith. You have unity. And you have the ability to stay submitted even as you succeed.

Money is a tool.

Purpose is the mission.

Unity is the power.

God is the source.

When God remains first and your marriage remains protected, wealth will not harm you. It will strengthen you. It will expand your influence. And it will position your family to impact generations with wisdom and grace.

This chapter is not the conclusion; it is an invitation. An invitation into a lifestyle where faith and wealth no longer compete, but collaborate. Where success does not erode the soul, and increase does not dilute devotion.

You are ready for this level of stewardship. Walk forward grounded, united, and confident in the God who leads you.

Closing Prayer

Father, in the mighty name of Jesus, we thank You for *every lesson, every revelation, and every seed planted through this journey.*

As a couple, we surrender our financial goals, our desires, and our dreams back to You. Lord, keep us grounded in Your presence. Let success never distract us from Your voice. Let increase never pull our hearts away from obedience. Let ambition never overshadow our unity.

Strengthen our marriage so that it reflects Your love. Guide our financial decisions so they align with purpose. Protect our hearts from pride, comparison, and materialism. Remind us daily that You, not money, are our source.

Father, give us wisdom beyond our years, discipline beyond our habits, and vision beyond our comfort. Cover our home with peace, provision, and divine strategy.

We declare that we will grow spiritually as we grow financially. We will stay grounded, grateful, and generous. We will build wealth without losing our souls. And we will walk boldly into the future You have designed for us.

Thank You for choosing us to carry this mantle of Kingdom wealth.

We seal this prayer with unity, faith, and expectation.

In Jesus' name, Amen.

ABOUT THE AUTHORS

Lolita and Van Brown are husband and wife, partners in purpose, and advocates for building wealth, love, and legacy with intention.

Lolita Brown is a devoted wife and mother to Ezekiel, Ziza, and Zayna Brown, as well as a trusted Financial Advisor and Wealth Educator with over 21 years of experience. Through her mentorship platform, **Manage My Wealth**, Lolita has helped individuals and families establish strong financial foundations, create multiple income streams, and build generational wealth rooted in discipline, stewardship, and vision. She also serves as a Marriage and Family Coach, guiding couples toward alignment in love, money, and purpose. Lolita's work bridges practical financial strategy with heart-centered transformation, empowering families to thrive for generations to come.

Van Brown is an author, teacher, and life coach known for his deep passion for helping individuals heal, rediscover purpose, and walk in wholeness. Born and raised in the Bahamas, Van is the Founder of **Celebration of Love**, a nonprofit organization dedicated to restoring lives and strengthening communities through love, mentorship, and service. For nearly two decades, his work has impacted youth and families both locally and internationally, especially in his homeland. Van is also the author of *Love Symptoms*, a powerful work that explores emotional health, relationships, and the transformative power of love. His greatest gift is love, and his life's mission is to help people become who God has always called them to be.

Together, Lolita and Van Brown have dedicated their lives to strengthening marriages, empowering families, and teaching others how to steward both love and money with wisdom and purpose. Through their marriage, their nonprofit Celebration of Love, and their shared message, they believe that true wealth is built when faith, finances, and family are aligned.

Married to Money is an extension of their journey, inviting couples to build not just financial success, but a legacy grounded in unity, intention, and love.

www.ingramcontent.com/pod-product-compliance
Lightning Source LLC
LaVergne TN
LVHW010703110826
845149LV00014B/3213